ENDING DISCRIMINATION IN
SPECIAL EDUCATION

ABOUT THE AUTHOR

Herbert Grossman has worked in special education as classroom teacher, clinical psychologist, and teacher trainer. He has been a member of the faculty of fourteen universities in the United States and abroad in the departments of special education, psychology, and psychiatry. And, he has guest-lectured at more than one hundred universities. Doctor Grossman has taught and consulted in Latin America, Africa, and Europe under the auspices of such organizations as UNESCO, the Fulbright Commission, Project Hope, and the International Foundation for Education and Self Help. He directed the multicultural and bilingual special education programs at San Jose State University for sixteen years. This is his sixth book about special education.

Second Edition

ENDING DISCRIMINATION IN SPECIAL EDUCATION

By

HERBERT GROSSMAN, Ph.D.

Charles C Thomas
PUBLISHER • LTD.
SPRINGFIELD • ILLINOIS • U.S.A.

Published and Distributed Throughout the World by

CHARLES C THOMAS • PUBLISHER, LTD.
2600 South First Street
Springfield, Illinois 62704

©2002 by CHARLES C THOMAS • PUBLISHER, LTD.

ISBN 0-398-07304-X

Library of Congress Catalog Card Number: 2002019183

With THOMAS BOOKS *careful attention is given to all details of man-
ufacturing and design. It is the Publisher's desire to present books that are sat-
isfactory as to their physical qualities and artistic possibilities and appropriate for their particular use.* THOMAS BOOKS *will be true to those laws
of quality that assure a good name and good will.*

Printed in the United States of America
CR-R-3

Library of Congress Cataloging-in-Publication Data

Grossman, Herbert, 1934-
    Ending discrimination in special education / by Herbert Grossman.--2nd ed.
        p. cm.
    Includes bibliographical references.
    ISBN 0-398-07304-X (paper)
    1. Special education--Social aspects--United States. 2. Discrimination in
education--United States. 3. Minorities--Education--United States. 4. Educational
equalization--United States. I. Title.

LC3981 .G757 2002
371.9'04--dc21

                                                                        2002019183

PREFACE

There are huge disparities in the school experiences and educational outcomes of the students in our special education system. For example, students without disabilities who are poor, non-European Americans, or immigrants continue to be misplaced in special education programs. Numerous students with disabilities who are limited English proficient, migrants, or homeless are denied the special education they merit. In addition, gifted and talented students from these backgrounds are especially likely to be deprived of the special education services they require.

Students with disabilities and gifts and talents from these backgrounds who are correctly placed in special education often receive services that are culturally inappropriate and ill suited to the socioeconomic, geographic, and other factors that shape the context of their lives. Students with disabilities who are limited English proficient or speak a nonstandard English dialect often experience an additional problem–linguistically inappropriate services.

The primary cause of these problems is the discriminatory practices that pervade our special education system. One of the main reasons why this discrimination exists is that special education is not special for all students. In recent years, most special education educators have been attempting to individualize their pedagogy to the disabilities, gifts, and talents of their students. Psychologists have been preparing reports that suggest how they may do so, and administrators have been attempting to provide them with the tools they need to accomplish this goal. However, the assessment, instruction, classroom management, and counseling approaches that are currently being employed are inappropriate for the many poor, non-European American, immigrant, refugee, migrant, rural, and limited English proficient students in our special education programs because they are designed for European American, middle- and upper-class, English proficient students.

Prejudice, usually unconscious, toward these students is a second major source of discrimination. Although some teachers may not be biased, most are. The referral and placement process is just one example of the many ways educators', psychologists', and school administrators' treatment of poor and certain non-European students reflects the biases that exist in the larger society. When teachers refer students for evaluation for possible placement in special education programs, they are more likely to refer poor students and students of color for placement in programs for students with disabilities and less likely to refer them to programs for the gifted and talented. When special education educators and psychologists evaluate these students they tend to judge their work, performance, intellectual abilities, and social skills to be lower than objective data would indicate. When selecting the most appropriate placement for students with the same behavioral and academic problems they are more likely to choose a special education program for non-European Americans and poor students and a regular education program for middle-class European American students. Moreover, when they choose a special education program for students, they are likely to recommend a more restrictive, custodial environment for non-European Americans and poor students than for middle-class European American students.

Ending Discrimination in Special Education explains the forces that create and maintain these and other discriminatory assessment, instructional, classroom management, and counseling approaches and describes what we can do to eliminate them. In this second edition I have added four new chapters that provide more detailed suggestions of how special education educators, psychologists, and others can avoid the discriminatory practices identified in the first edition. I have also examined gender discrimination in special education at greater length. And I have included the finding of research that has become available since the publication of the first edition.

The book includes an introduction and seven chapters. The Introduction describes the harmful effects of discrimination in special education. Chapters 1 and 2 discuss prejudice in special education and suggest how special education educators and others who work with exceptional students can eliminate it. Chapter 3 details the culturally, contextually, linguistically, and gender discriminatory special education services many students receive. Chapters 4 through 6 explain how special education educators can adapt their assessment, instruction, and classroom management approaches to students' diverse characteristics. Chapter 7 describes the obstacles we must overcome to end discrimination and achieve equality in special education and provides suggestions for how to do so.

The ideas, suggestions, and conclusions expressed in the book are controversial. However, I believe that it is important to tell the truth. I do not want to add my voice to those calling for halfhearted changes in our special education approaches. I want to lay out the problems and their solutions as I see them and as research dictates.

I have written *Ending Discrimination in Special Education* with two groups of readers in mind. One group is the special education educators, administrators, and psychologists currently working in special education. This book is well suited to the needs of these in-service personnel. The second group are special education educators, administrators, and psychologists in training and regular education teachers in training who need to acquire the competencies necessary to succeed with all the students with disabilities, gifts, and talents who will be included in their classrooms. To reach this second audience, I have designed the book so that it can be used as a supplementary text in the introductory special education course offered to preservice special education educators, and in the mainstreaming/full inclusion course taken by regular education teachers in training.

HERBERT GROSSMAN, PH.D.

INTRODUCTION

The enormous disparities between the school experiences and educational outcomes of students of color, poor, immigrant, refugee, rural, and limited English proficient exceptional students, and their European American middle- and upper-class peers testifies to the fact that they do not receive a just share of the special education pie or fair treatment in the special education system. They are still misrepresented–over- and underenrolled–in special education programs. Those who are misplaced in special education are denied the kind of education they would profit from in regular education programs. Those who are not identified as eligible for special education are deprived of the services their disabilities and gifts and talents require.

Although some school districts have cleaned up their acts, poor students and students of color, especially those who are African Americans, Hispanic Americans, Native Americans, immigrants, refugees, or migrants have been and are still grossly misrepresented in those special education programs in which placement decisions are subject to assessment bias–programs for students with learning disabilities, behavior disorders, mild developmental disabilities, and gifts and talents versus those for students with physical or sensory disabilities (1-11). Although, the type of misrepresentation they experience differs from state to state and from school district to school district, in general African American, Hispanic American, Native American, and poor students are still underrepresented in programs for the gifted and talented and overrepresented in special education classes for students with behavior disorders, learning disabilities, serious emotional problems, communication disorders, and mild developmental disabilities.

Asian and Pacific Island American students tend to be underrepresented in programs for students with learning disabilities, serious emotional problems, and behavior disorders and overrepresented in programs for students with speech disorders. In fact, in some school districts as many as 50 percent of the Asian and Pacific Island American students receiving special education services are in such programs.

African Americans experience the greatest overrepresentation. Although they account for only 12 percent of the elementary and secondary school population, they constitute 28 percent of the total enrollment in special education programs for students with disabilities.

Students of color who are also limited English proficient are even more likely to be misrepresented in special education programs. A number of bilingual special education programs for limited-English proficient gifted and talented students have been initiated in recent years. However, on a nationwide basis these students have and continue to be underrepresented in such programs because there are so few bilingual special educators.

To some educators, underrepresentation of limited English proficient students in programs for students with behavior disorders, emotional problems, learning disabilities, and mild developmental disabilities is an improvement because it signifies that fewer of them are being misplaced in programs for students with disabilities. However, many poor immigrant and refugee students need these kinds of special education services because of the extreme physical and psychological deprivation they experienced before they emigrated to the United States.

There is also considerable gender misrepresentation in special education (12-17). Males are much more likely to be enrolled in programs for students with developmental, behavioral, emotional, and learning disabilities. There are two reasons for this disparity. Males, especially poor African Americans, Hispanic Americans, and Native Americans, are often misplaced in these programs. Moreover, female students with cognitive or emotional problems are frequently denied the special education services they require.

Students who are correctly placed in special education often receive services that are culturally inappropriate and ill suited to socioeconomic, geographic, and other factors that shape the context of their lives. In addition, students who are limited English proficient or speak a nonstandard English dialect often experience a third problem—linguistically inappropriate services.

Although researchers have studied the effectiveness of the special education services provided to exceptional students, very few of them have been interested in studying whether these services are equally effective with poor and middle- and upper-class students, European American students and students of color, and English proficient and limited English proficient students. Most of the programs specifically designed to deliver culturally, contextually, and linguistically appropriate services to students of color or limited English proficient students with disabilities or gifts and talents are effective, at least to some degree. However, the majority of special education programs are not designed with the needs of poor students, students of color, and limited English proficient students in mind. Studies of these programs indicate they are not effective (18-23). With very few exceptions, African American, Hispanic American, Native American, and poor students in these programs earn lower grades and score lower on standardized tests than their European American middle-class peers. They are also less likely to be returned to mainstream classes, to graduate from high school, to continue their studies after high school, to achieve vocational success, to be employed, or to earn a good living.

Poor students are especially likely to do badly in special education regardless of their ethnic background. The dropout rate for the poorest students is almost four times as great as that of students in the highest socioeconomic class group.

Gender differences in the effectiveness of special education have also been observed. However, so few studies have considered the issue, that it would be unwise to attempt to make any generalizations at this point in time (14, 17, 24-27).

These facts paint a sorry picture of the inequality in special education. It is time to face these facts and do something about them.

REFERENCES

These references discuss the misrepresentation of African American, Asian and Pacific Island American, Hispanic American, Native American, immigrant, refuges, migrant, and homeless students in special education:

1. Burnette, J. (1998). *Reducing the Disproportionate Representation of Minority Students in Special Education.* ERIC ED 417 501.
2. Cahalane, B. H. (1996). *The Disproportionate Representation of Minorities in Rural Special Education Programs and What Can Be Done about It.* ERIC ED 408 119.
3. Cline, T., & Frederickson, N. (1999). Identification and assessment of dyslexia in bi/multilingual children. *International Journal of Bilingual Education and Bilingualism, 2*(2), 81-93.

4. Coulter, W. A. (1996). *Alarming or Disarming?: The Status of Ethnic Differences within Exceptionalites.* ERIC ED 394 257.

5. Ford, D. Y. (1998). The underrepresentation of minority students in gifted education: Problems and promises in recruitment and retention. *Journal of Special Education, 32*(1), 4-14.

6. Individuals with Disabilities Education Act (20) U. S. C., Sections 1400-1485.

7. McNamara, B. E. (1998). *Learning Disabilities: Appropriate Practices for a Diverse Population. SUNY Series, Youth Social Services, Schooling, and Public Policy.* Albany: State University of New York Press.

8. Oswald, D. P., Coutinho, M. J., Best, A. M., & Singh, N. N. (1999). Ethnic representation in special education: The influence of ethnic and demographic variables. *Journal of Special Education, 32*(4), 194-206.

9. Pilla, T. V. (1999). *Alaska Natives and Other Minorities in the Special Education Programs of Four Alaskan School Districts.* ERIC ED 449 957.

10. Russo, C. J., & Talbert-Johnson, C. (1997). The overrepresentation of African American children in special education: The resegregation of educational programming? *Education and Urban Society, 29*(2), 136-148.

11. Wright III, D.E. Hirling, M. W., England, & R. E. (1998). *The Politics of Second Generation Discrimination in American Indian Education: Incidence Explanation and Mitigating Strategies.* ERIC ED 420 468.

These references document gender differences in special education enrollment:

12. Anderson, K. G. (1997). Gender bias and special education referrals. *Annals of Dyslexia, 47*, 151-162.

13. Caseau, D. L., Luckasson, R., G. Kroth, R.L. (1994). Services for girls with serious emotional disturbance: A case of gender bias? *Behavior Disorders, 20*(1), 51-60.

14. Lichtenstein, S. (1996). Gender differences in the education and employment of young adults: Implications for special education. *Remedial and Special Education, 17*(1), 4-20.

15. McIntyre, T., & Tong, V. (1998). Where the boys are: Do cross-gender misunderstandings of language use and behavior patterns contribute to the overrepresentation of males in programs for students with emotional and behavioral disorders? *Education and Treatment of Children, 2*(3), 321-332.

16. Wenger, B., Kaye, H. S., & LaPlante, M. P. (1996). *Disabilities among Children. Disabilities Statistics Abstract, Number 15.* ERIC ED 396 466.

17. Young, G., Kim, H. J., & Gerber, P. J. (1999). Bias and learning disabilities: School age and long term consequences for females. *Learning Disabilities: A Multidisciplinary Journal, 9*(3), 107-114.

These references provide evidence that students of color and poor students who attend programs that are not designed to provide them with culturally, contextually, and linguistically appropriate special education services do poorly:

18. Blackorby, J., & Kortering, L. J. (1991). A third of our youth? A look at the problem of high school dropout among students with mild handicaps. *Journal of Special Education, 25* (1), 102-113.

19. Harnisch, D. L., Lichtenstein, S. J., & Langford, J. B. (1989). *Digest on Youth in Transition Volume 1.* ERIC ED 279 118.

20. Palmateer, R. (1988). *Educare: Evaluation of a Transition Program for Culturally Disadvantaged and Educationally Handicapped Youth. Executive Summary.* ERIC ED 305 791.

21. Rice, M. M. (2000). Transition study reveals the plight of special needs students. *Rural Educator, 21*(2), 33-36.

22. Wagner, M., & Blackorby, J. (1996). Transition from high school to work of college: How special education students fare. *Future of Children, 6*(1), 103-120.

23. Wyche Sr., L. G., (1989). The Tenth Annual Report to Congress: Taking a significant step in the right direction. *Exceptional Children, 56*(1), 14-16.

These references deal with gender differences in the results of special education services:

24. Dannenbring, G., & Lanning-Ventura, S. (1985). *Academic Growth Made By Learning Disabled Students.* ERIC ED 280 202.

25. Gruenhagen, K. A. (1993). Appalachian special education students dropping out of school: Looking at the whos and whys. *Rural Special Education Quarterly, 12*(2), 14-20.

26. Harnisch, D. L., & Fisher, A. T. (1989). *Digest on Youth in Transition.* ERIC ED 318 163.

27. Porter, M. E. (1988). *How Vocational Teachers Rate Classroom Performance of Students with Mild Handicaps Using Curriculum-Based Vocational Assessment Procedures.* ERIC ED 308 639.

ACKNOWLEDGMENTS

I want to express my gratitude to Charles C Thomas, Publisher for their support of my work over many years and to professors Janette Klinger and Mary Franklin for the many suggestions they made for improving the first edition. As always, my wife read every word of every draft of both editions and made invaluable recommendations for their improvement.

CONTENTS

Page

Preface v
Introduction ix

Chapter

1. PREJUDICE AND DISCRIMINATION 3

2. ELIMINATING PREJUDICE AND DISCRIMINATION 12

3. DISCRIMINATORY SPECIAL EDUCATION SERVICES 20

4. NON-DISCRIMINATORY ASSESSMENT 45

5. NON-DISCRIMINATORY INSTRUCTION 69

6. NON-DISCRIMINATORY CLASSROOM MANAGEMENT . 85

7. OVERCOMING OBSTACLES TO CHANGE 105

ENDING DISCRIMINATION IN SPECIAL EDUCATION

Chapter 1

PREJUDICE AND DISCRIMINATION

One of the main, if not the main cause of inequality in special education is prejudice. Prejudice towards people who are different than we are is a pandemic disease of humankind. Witness the tension, conflicts, and sometimes even outright wars caused by religious differences in Northern Ireland, India; by ethnic differences in Iraq, the former Yugoslavia, the Philippines, China, the former Soviet Union, Rwanda, and Burundi; socioeconomic class in Great Britain; by skin color differences in South Africa, Australia, Great Britain, and Mexico; by language differences in Canada, India; and by whether individuals are immigrants or native-born citizens in Germany and other western European countries just to name a few.

Prejudice and discrimination contribute to disproportionate representation in the special education programs of most developed countries (1-3). For example, in Great Britain, non-English language speaking students, especially those from Afro Caribbean backgrounds are overrepresented in programs for students with developmental and behavior disorders. In the other western European countries "minority pupils" especially bilingual and Muslim students are overrepresented. In eastern Europe countries, it is the Romani (Gypsy) children who are misplaced in special education.

> Gypsy children from the first grades were automatically stuck into special schools for the mentally handicapped. They weren't retarded, but they were handicapped: they didn't speak the language, and the deficiency had become a widespread excuse for segregation and indeed incarceration. (3, p. 163)

It seems that we humans have an inborn potential to reject and mistreat people who are different than we are. We don't have to reject and mistreat them, but we have the latent capacity to do so. There is no reason to assume that Americans, who are members of the human race, should have escaped this universal potentiality. The evidence consistently indicates that we have not. And that includes our special education system as well.

My first experience with prejudice in special education occurred when I was teaching in a residential treatment center for emotionally disturbed and delinquent adolescents. Somewhere around 90 to 95 percent of the students were European Americans; less than 10 percent were African Americans or Hispanic Americans. Whenever, and it wasn't very often, a white female would pair off with a black male, the staff would discuss the diagnostic implications of her behavior. For most of my colleagues, there were only two possible reasons for her behavior. Either she was rebelling against society by breaking a sacred taboo or she felt too inferior to believe that she could attract a white male. Very few staff members could conceive of the possibility that she just liked him.

I do not think things have changed very much since then. Ask yourself these three questions: What assumptions would a group of European American teachers make about the reasons why an African American high school student would hang out with a group of European American students? What assumptions would they make about the reasons why a European American male student would hang out with a group of African American male high school students? What would they think about a European American female student who hung out with a group of African American male students?

In 1964, I was fortunate to be given the chance to start an experimental day treatment school for inner-city adolescents who were incarcerated and awaiting placement in correctional facilities, residential treatment centers, or mental hospitals. The director of the agency who gave me the opportunity was a visionary. He retired two years later and was replaced by someone with a more traditional approach.

After I had been running the program for almost three years, the new director and the chief psychiatrist of the agency came to have a look at what we were doing. They read the students' records, observed the classes, and interviewed the teachers and therapists. A couple of weeks later, they said that they wanted me to return six students to the courts. They were too dangerous to be allowed to remain in the community, I was told. And, if they caused trouble in the community, the agency and the program would be held responsible.

But they were all doing well, I protested. None of them had gotten into trouble, and they all had been in the program for at least a year. My protests had no effect. The agency still wanted me to get rid of the six students. I refused. First they insisted, then they threatened, then they fired me and returned the students to the court themselves. The students were all African Americans or Hispanic Americans. Not a European American among them.

I have often thought about what those kids must have felt when they were punished even though they had been behaving well, getting better, and overcoming their problems. I also thought a great deal about why the chief psychiatrist and the director of the agency treated them so unjustly. I came to the conclusion that neither of them came to the school to look for African American and Hispanic American kids to ship back to court. I have no reason to believe that they hated African Americans or Hispanic Americans. I believe that they didn't know anything about kids of color. And not understanding them they were afraid of them. They probably were trying to protect society and the agency's good name, but they picked the wrong kids to protect them from. There is no doubt in my mind, that if those kids had been European Americans they would have had a better shake from society and its agents.

There is also little doubt in my mind that the same thing would easily happen today. As we will see later, students of color with disabilities are still more likely to be placed in more restrictive custodial settings than European American students.

All the students that attended the experimental day treatment school were evaluated by a court or agency psychologist. The results of their evaluations were a lesson in biased assessment. All but one of the Hispanic American and African American students had I.Q. scores that would have qualified them for a program for the developmentally disabled (mentally retarded). All of the European American students had normal or higher I.Q. scores. As you might expect, none of the so-called retarded students was actually retarded. If they had been retarded, they would not have been able to outsmart us so often.

Times have not changed very much. African Americans, Hispanic Americans, Native Americans, and other students of color are still assessed with biased instruments. And, they are still misplaced in programs for the developmentally disabled and denied access to programs for students with gifts and talents.

Most educators believe that they are not biased against students of color and poor students. However, although many teachers are not biased, many others are. Teachers', psychologists', and school administrators' treatment of poor students and many groups of students of color reflects the biases that exist in the larger society (4-23).

Teachers' expectations of their students tend to be prejudicial. Many special education educators and special education educators in training expect European American middle-class students to do better academically than most groups of students of color and poor students. Even when students' achievement test scores, grades, and school histories would predict otherwise, they tend to believe European American middle-class students are more intelligent. They also expect many groups of students of color, especially African Americans, to be more disruptive and deviant than European Americans.

Because we often think we see what we expect to see, these biased teacher expectations become self-fulfilling prophesies. And they contribute to the lack of African American and Hispanic American students in programs for the gifted and talented and to their overrepresentation in programs for students with behavior disorders.

Teachers tend to evaluate students of color behavior in a biased manner. When teachers evaluate the severity or deviancy of students' behavior problems, they judge the exact same transgressions as more severe or deviant when they are committed by African Americans than when they are committed by European Americans. African American students who are seen as fun loving, happy, cooperative, energetic, and ambitious by their African American teachers are viewed as talkative, lazy, fun loving high-strung, and frivolous by their European American teachers. This too contributes to the lack of African Americans and Hispanic Americans in programs for students with gifts and talents and their overrepresentation in programs for students with behavior disorders.

When teachers and school psychologists refer students to special education programs, evaluate them for possible placement in special education programs, or select the most appropriate placement for them, their evaluations of students of color and poor students are biased. Teachers are more likely to refer poor students and students of color for evaluation for possible placement in programs for students with disabilities and less likely to refer them to programs for the gifted and talented. When evaluating them, they tend to judge these students' work, performance, intellectual abilities, and social skills to be lower than objective data would indicate.

When selecting the most appropriate placement for students with the same behavioral and academic problems, educators and psychologists tend to choose a special education program for students of color and poor students and a regular education program for middle-class European American students. When they choose a special education program for students, they are more likely to select a program for students with mild developmental disabilities for students of color and poor students and a learning disabilities program for middle-class European American students. They also are more prone to recommend a more restrictive, custodial environment for students of color and poor students than for middle-class European American students.

Being poor and African American places students at even greater risk to be on the receiving end of teacher bias. Teachers are also more likely to refer poor, African American students to programs for students with disabilities and less likely to refer them to programs for the gifted and talented, and they are 3.5 times more likely to identify them as developmentally disabled than their European American peers.

> Professionals in education may view cultural differences among Black students as indicators of deficiencies. This perception can lead to a student being identified as being below normal or abnormal on measures of adaptive behavior and social development. Scoring low or scoring as abnormal on these measures can in turn lead to placement in classrooms for emotionally disturbed and educable mentally retarded pupils. (19, p. 21)

Teachers evaluate Asian and Pacific Island American students in a biased manner. There appear to be two reasons for this. First, believing that all are good students, teachers fail to notice their academic problems and neglect to refer students with learning disabilities for special education evaluation. Second, because Asian and Pacific Island American students tend to internalize their emotional problems rather than act them out, their suffering is less obvious and less disruptive than that of students who act out their problems. As a result, they are less likely to be noticed by teachers or to be referred for special education services.

Teachers tend to treat students of color and poor students unfairly. In comparison to European American students, teachers praise African Americans less and criticize them more. The praise they give them is more likely to be routine, rather than feedback for a particular achievement or behavior. And when teachers praise them for a specific behavior, it is more likely to be qualified ("Your work is almost good enough to be put on the board") or in the case of females, more likely to be for good behavior than for academic work.

Teachers interact less with African Americans, especially males, than with European American students, give them less attention, and are less likely to respond to their questions or to direct questions to them. Unlike the preferential treatment many teachers give their brightest European American students, they give bright African American students, especially females, the least attention and criticize them the most. Although teachers typically demonstrate considerable concern and interest in European American females' academic work, they often pay less attention to African American female students' academic work than to their social behavior.

Educators tend to use different classroom management approaches with African American and European American students. They spend more time on the lookout for possible misbehavior by African American students, especially males. When male students misbehave, educators are prone to criticize African American males' behavior and to use more severe punishments including corporal punishment and suspension with them. When females misbehave, teachers treat African Americans more harshly than European Americans.

Teachers relate to Hispanic American students in a discriminatory manner. Although Hispanic American students tend to prefer more positive reinforcement and feedback from their teachers than most European American students, teachers praise them less often and give them less positive feedback when they answer correctly or perform well. Teachers are also less likely to encourage them when they need encouragement, to accept their ideas, and to direct questions to them.

Poor students also receive unfair treatment in school. Beginning in primary school, teachers give them fewer rewards and social and instructional contacts, but more disciplinary and control contacts. In addition, when they discipline poor students, teachers in schools that serve predominantly poor students are more likely to endorse or use corporal punishments, verbal punishments, or suspension than teachers in schools attended by middle-class students.

When I ask myself why special education educators and others continue to treat students in such discriminatory ways, I find three explanations. First, as stated earlier, prejudice and discrimination are part of the human condition. We seemed to be programmed to discriminate against people who do not belong to our group, or who look, talk, think, or act differently from us. Prejudice and discrimination are an ever-present danger against which we constantly must be vigilant.

Second, much of our prejudice is unconscious. Wanting to see ourselves in a good light, we hide our prejudice from ourselves. Sometimes, we purposely do not notice that we call on one group of students more than another, expect more from one group than another, or reward and punish one group more than another. At other times, we allow ourselves to become aware of the different ways we treat different groups of students but justify and rationalize our inappropriate behavior. We do this by attributing characteristics such as linguistic inadequacy, aggressiveness, cultural inferiority, laziness, and other prejudicial stereotypes that pervade our society to the students we discriminate against, thereby convincing ourselves that these characteristics justify the manner in which we treat them. Being unaware of the discriminatory way we treat students and/or justifying it, we have no need to change our behavior.

Finally, many teachers discriminate against students who are unlike them because they fear them. This is clearly true of the many European American teachers who keep African American students at a distance, avoid calling on them, remain on the lookout for signs that they are about to misbehave and cause trouble, use strict and severe forms of discipline with them, and so on. European American teachers are aware of the ways in which African Americans, Hispanic Americans, Native Americans, and poor people in general were and continue to be treated by our society. They know about the unemployment, poverty, racism, discrimination, and so on that these students and their families experience. They sense the resentment, anger, and mistrust these students harbor toward the European American establishment that treats them so unjustly. They are well aware of the periodic angry explosions that have rocked our society when these groups could not take any more. Is it any wonder that down deep they are afraid of how their students may react to them?

REFERENCES

Special education inequality in European countries is described in these publications:

1. Diniz, F. A. (1999). Race and special educational needs in the 1990s. *British Journal of Special Education, 26*(4), 213-217.
2.. Fonseca, I. (1996). *Bury Me Standing: The Gypsies and Their Journey.* New York: Vintage Books.
3. Organization for Economic Cooperation and Development. (1987). *Immigrant Children at School.* Paris: OECD.

The references describe teachers' and psychologists' biased expectation evaluation, and treatment of students:

4. Campos, F. (1983). *The Attitudes and Expectations of Student Teachers and Cooperating Teachers Toward Students in Predominantly Mexican American Schools: A Qualitative Data Perspective.* ERIC ED 234 026.
5.Cooley, S. (1995). *Suspensions/Expulsions of Regular and Special Education Students in Kansas: A Report to the Kansas State Board of Education.* ERIC ED 395 403.
6. Collier, C. (1986). *The Referral of Hispanic Children to Special Education: A Comparison of Acculturation and Education Characteristics of Referred and Nonreferred Culturally and Linguistically Different Children.* ERIC ED 271 954.
7. Dao, M. (1991). Designing assessment procedures for educationally at-risk Southeast Asian-American students. *Journal of Learning Disabilities, 24*(10), 594-601, 629.
8. Fasko, D., Grubb, D. J., & Osborne, S. J. (1995). *An Analysis of Disciplinary Suspensions.* ERIC ED 393 169.
9. Fiore, T., & Reynolds, K. S. (1996). *Analysis of Discipline Issues in Special Education.* ERIC ED 425 607.
10. Grant, L. (1984). Black females' "place" in desegregated classrooms. *Sociology of Education, 57,* 98-110.
11. Grant, L. (1985). Race-gender status, classroom interaction, and children's socialization in elementary school. In L. C. Wilkinson & C. B. Marrett (Eds.), *Gender Influences in Classroom Interaction.* New York: Academic.
12. Gregory, J. (1995). The crime of punishment: Racial and gender disparities in the use of corporal punishment in U.S. public schools. *Journal of Negro Education, 64*(4), 54-62.

13. Grossman, H., & Grossman, S. (1994). *Gender Issues in Education.* Needham, MA: Allyn & Bacon.
14. Handy, A. J. (1999). *Ethnocentric and Black Students with Disabilities: Bridging the Cultural Gap, Volume I.* ERIC ED 430 356.
15. Individuals with Disabilities Education Act (20 U. S. C., Sections 1400-1485; Education of the Handicapped Act Amendments of 1990).
16. Ishi-Jordan, S. (1992). *Effects of Students' Racial or Ethnic Background on Teacher Expectations and Intervention Selection for Problem Behaviors.* Paper presented at the Topical Conference on Cultural and Linguistically Diverse Exceptional Children, Minneapolis.
17. Meier, T., & Brown, C. R. (1994). The color of inclusion. *Journal of Emotional and Behavioral Problems, 3*(3), 15-18.
18. Richardson, R. C., & Evans, E. T. (1991). *Empowering Teachers to Eliminate Corporal Punishment in the Schools.* Paper presented at the annual conference of the National Black Child Developmental Institute. Washington, DC,.
19. Serwata, T., Dove, T., & Hodges, W. (986). Black students in special education: Issues and implications for community involvement. *Negro Educational Review, 37*(1), 17-26.
20. Shaw, S. R., & Braden, J. P. (1990). Race and gender bias in the administration of corporal punishment. *School Psychology Review, 19*(3), 378-383.
21. Skiba, R., Russell, J., Peterson, R. L., & Williams, T. (1997). Office referrals and suspensions: Disciplinary intervention in middle school. *Education and Treatment of Children, 20* (3), 295-315.
22. Van Keulen, J. E. (1995). Why is there an overrepresentation of African Americans in special education classes? *College of Education Review, 7,* 76-88.
23. Yao, E. L. (1987). Asian-immigrants students–Unique problems that hamper learning. *NASSP Bulletin, 71*(503), 82-88.

Chapter 2

ELIMINATING PREJUDICE AND DISCRIMINATION

Prejudice in special education takes many forms (1-6). Many special education educators and psychologists are convinced that some students of color, especially African Americans, Hispanic Americans, and poor students tend to be less intelligent than European American middle-class students. The following quotes are representative of this position. Shockley and Jensen maintain that different groups identifiable by their skin color inherit different amounts/types of intelligence.

> Nature has color-coded groups of individuals so that statistically reliable predictions of their adaptability to intellectually rewarding and effective lives can easily be made and profitably be used by the pragmatic man-in-the-street. (1, p. 375)

> The most parsimonious hypothesis—one that would comprehend virtually all the established facts about the white-black IQ difference without the need to postulate any environmental factors besides those that are known to affect IQ and on which blacks in general are less advantaged—is that something between one-half and three-fourths of the average IQ difference is attributable to genetic factors, and the remainder to environmental factors and their interaction with genetic differences. (2, p. 227)

Herrenstein claims that because our society is a meritocracy in which all people have an equal opportunity to succeed, those that do not succeed lack either the ability or motivation to do so. So those who remain in the working class, especially those who are below the poverty level and those who do poorly in school lack either the motivation or the intelligence to do better. "1. If differences in mental abilities are inherited, and 2. if success requires these abilities, and 3. if earnings and prestige depend on success, 4. then social standing (which reflects earnings and prestige) will be based to some extent on inherited differences among people" (3, pp. 58-59).

The claim that different ethnic groups and socioeconomic classes inherit different kinds or amounts of intelligence is based on two incorrect assumptions: American society is a meritocracy and skin-color groups and socioeconomic classes inherit different amounts/kinds of intelligences. The United States is not a meritocracy. Schools do not provide a level playing field that enables all students to achieve their potential. Instead of being designed to provide all students the knowledge and skills they need to succeed in life regardless of their ethnic and socioeconomic-class backgrounds, schools are biased against the very groups that do so poorly. Schools that serve primarily middle- and upper-class European American students have many more resources than schools who serve primarily non-European and poor students. Per-pupil expenditures for public schools serving students in poor and non-European neighborhoods are considerably below those for schools in European American middle-class areas. In part, this is because local and state governments spend less money on them. Moreover, because schools in poor neighborhoods are underfunded, they often have to settle for the least adequately prepared teachers. Thus, there is no justification for believing that poor students who do not do well in school and families that remain poor or below the poverty level are responsible for the state of affairs they find themselves in.

Skin-color groups and socioeconomic classes do not differ in their intellectual abilities. The differences observed between the scores of European American middle-class students and African American, Hispanic American, and poor students on so-called intelligence tests are due to test bias, not real differences in intellectual ability. As is seen in Chapter 4, the tests used to measure these intellectual abilities do not measure intelligence nor predict how students will perform in school. The content, language, and format of standardized tests that purport to measure intelligence are biased. They are poor predictors of students' of color and poor students' academic achievement or their learning potentials. Comparisons of the assumed intelligence of different groups based on the results of biased instruments and assessors are invalid, misleading, and harmful. They do not explain or justify ethnic or socioeconomic-class differences in students' achievement or their enrollment in special education programs.

Some special education educators and psychologists believe that poor students, particularly those from African American and Hispanic American backgrounds are brought up in disadvantaged cultures that deprive them of the skills, attitudes, and behavior patterns necessary to succeed in school that students who grow up in the "superior" European American middle-class culture possess (4, 5). For example, the language of educationally disadvantaged students is supposedly inadequate because the environments in which they grow up provide few opportunities to use language in cognitively complex ways. These deficits are attributed to parents who provide children poor language models and spend insufficient time communicating with children.

Students of color, especially those from African American, Native American, and Hispanic American poor backgrounds, are thought to have poor self-concepts and low self-esteem from a variety of causes. They supposedly lack successful role models in their families and communities to identify with. Repeated failure in school and other competitive situations is assumed to lower their self-image. They are believed to suffer a loss of self-esteem when they compare their lives and living conditions with those of their middle-class and European American peers. They supposedly have low educational and career aspirations.

These ideas have been shown to be false (4, 5). Many of the characteristics that are attributed to cultural disadvantage are actually the result of poor peoples' inability to afford and obtain the resources available to the middle- and upper classes and the disadvantages many poor immigrants experience because of their limited English proficiency. Poor parents want their children to do well in school, however many of them are unemployed, underemployed, underpaid, undereducated, and unable to provide their children with the childhood experiences needed to prepare them for school or the educational and financial support they require to assist their youngsters during their educational careers. Moreover, local and state governments spend less money on schools that serve predominantly poor students. If society provided more support for programs designed to assist and supplement poor parents' efforts such as day care and preschool programs, programs that prepare parents to participate in their children's education, and programs that provide students with access to educational programs including the added resources they require to compete successfully with their more economically advantaged peers, the effects of so-called cultural disadvantage would disappear. Until then, educators should have a realistic picture of both the kinds of educational support and assistance parents can provide their children and the way their financial situation affects their children's functioning in school. Educators should adapt their educational approaches to these realities. Until this happens, many children of poor parents will continue to fail in regular education. They will be misplaced into special education programs because educators mistakenly believe that the learning and behavior problems their economic disadvantages create are caused by learning or developmental disabilities.

There is no evidence that genetically determined differences in intellectual ability contribute significantly to ethnic and socioeconomic-class educational disparities or that ethnic groups and socioeconomic classes inherit different intellectual potentials. Differences that have been observed occur because current methods of evaluating intelligence are biased and because our imperfect society has not yet achieved the assumptions underlying the meritocracy theory.

CORRECTING BIASES

Many professionals who work with exceptional students are unaware of their prejudices. Wanting to see themselves in a good light, they hide their prejudice from themselves. They do not notice that they call on one group of students more than another, expect more from one group than another, or reward and punish one group more than another. Some overcompensate for their prejudices. They praise students who belong to a different ethnic or socioeconomic group more than they do students who share their background, but they unknowingly treat them negatively by giving them less nonverbal positive attention, maintaining a greater distance from them, touching them less often, and providing them with less positive feedback when they answer questions correctly and fewer helpful hints when they call on them to answer questions.

If you are concerned that you may be unaware of your prejudices, you can evaluate your assumptions about your students' motives, your expectations for them, your relationships with them, and the assessment, instructional, and classroom management techniques you use with them to see whether you are unknowingly acting in a discriminatory way. For example, list the students in your class alphabetically and write down your expectations for each of them in terms of their behavior, achievement, goals, and so on. Then divide students into ethnic, linguistic, and socioeconomic-class groups and compare what you have written about the different groups. You can also ask yourself whether your expect students of color and poor students to achieve less and/or misbehave more than their test scores, grades, and previous performance would indicate. You may find that you evaluate their work objectively, or you may discover that your students' skin color, ethnicity, or socioeconomic background influence your conclusions (7).

Ask a colleague to assist you. Ask the colleague to observe your teaching and to compare the way you relate to different groups of students by studying your behavior. Your colleague can observe how often you call on students who do and do not volunteer, assign students to particular chores, praise students' work, assist students who are having difficulty answering questions by asking them leading questions, giving them hints, and so on and so on. Then the colleague can compare the results for different groups of students such as European Americans, students of color, poor students and middle-class students.

Ask a colleague to evaluate some of your students' work that is difficult to judge objectively (essay questions or a writing sample rather than a math problem or a multiple choice answer). Compare your colleague's evaluations with your own to see if your evaluations of particular groups of students are biased.

Examine your course content and the materials you are using to identify any bias that needs to be corrected. This list of sources of bias is a good way to discover whether like many special education educators, you have overemphasized the European American culture at the expense of the other cultures in our pluralistic society.

1. representing certain groups in an unflattering or demeaning manner: Hispanic Americans are lazy, African Americans are on welfare
2. overgeneralizing: African American families are always headed by females, Hispanic American always have many children; gang members are only African Americans or Hispanic Americans
3. omitting or underrepresenting people of color

4. stereotyping: studious Asian and Pacific Island Americans, athletic African Americans
5. assigning certain ethnic groups traditional and stereotypic roles that imply that they have limited abilities and potential, or are less valuable to society: European Americans perform leadership roles, take the initiative, play the key roles in solving problems, give aid and assistance and people of color are their helpers and the recipients of their assistance
6. omitting the roles of people of color in history, their contributions to science and literature, and so on
7. presenting only a European American perspective on such issues as wars and other conflicts between groups, calling Native American victories massacres and their defeats battles
8. presenting problems such as drug abuse, poverty, homelessness, and crime as if they were restricted to people of color
9. glossing over or ignoring such controversial or troublesome issues as slavery, oppression, poverty, prejudice, injustice
10. describing families as two-parent families living in suburban middle-class neighborhoods in which the father goes to work in a suit and the mother stays home
11. employing only middle-class standards of success such as a college degree and working as a professional, executive, or entrepreneur

Use a multicultural approach to include students' cultures in the curriculum. Teach students about their foods, clothing, stories, legends, dances, and arts. Select textbooks and other educational materials that include pictures of and stories about different ethnic groups. Listen to the music of different ethnic groups, discuss and celebrate their holidays, and note their historical and current contributions. Encourage students to bring to class things such as pictures, foods, games, photos, jewelry, money, musical instruments from home.

Do these and other multicultural activities on a regular basis as part of the ongoing curriculum and not only in special units or only on special occasions. "Setting aside a month for black history or women's history seems strange and artificial to most students regardless of color. These children aren't naive. What are the other seven months: White Male History Month?" (8, p. 14).

Be sure that what you include about students' cultures is not superficial stereotypes. Merely celebrating special days, learning about selected heroes, eating ethnic foods, and building tepees and igloos does not help students understand the experiences, attitudes, problems, lifestyles, and so on of different groups. Focus more on these real-life current problems.

> Focusing on the strange and exotic traits and characteristics of ethnic groups is likely to reinforce stereotypes and misconceptions. The making of tepees does not reveal anything significant about contemporary American Indian values, cultures, or experiences. It merely adds to the classical Indian stereotype, which is so pervasive on television and in the wider society. Rather than focus on the exotic characteristics of ethnic groups the teacher should emphasize the common needs which all human groups share, such as the need to explain the unknown and the need for artistic expression, and the diverse ways in which American ethnic groups have solved the problems of survival. (9, p. 86)

The study of Mexican-American food or of native American tepees will not help students develop a sophisticated understanding of Mexican-American culture and of the tremendous cultural diversity among native Americans. (6, p. 533)

REFERENCES

These authors maintain that certain groups are less intelligent than others:

1. Shockley, W. (1971). Models, mathematics, and the moral obligation to diagnose the origins of Negro IQ deficits. *Review of Educational Research, 41*(4), 369-377.
2. Jensen, A. R. (1981). *Straight Talk about Mental Tests.* New York: Free Press.
3. Herrenstein, R. J. (1973). *IQ in the Meritocracy.* Boston: Little, Brown.

These references provide evidence that refutes the ideas propounded by Herrenstein, Jensen, and Shockley, and some special educators and psychologists:

4. Grossman, H. (1998). *Achieving Educational Equality: Assuring All Students an Equal Opportunity in School.* Springfield, IL: Charles C Thomas Publisher, Ltd.
5. Grossman, H. (1995) *Special Education in a Diverse Society.* Springfield, IL: Charles C Thomas Publisher, Ltd.

Suggestions for identifying and correcting bias are included in these references:

6. Banks, J. A. (1987). Social studies, ethnic diversity, and social change. *Elementary School Journal, 87*(5), 531-543.

7. Bondy, E., & Ross, D. D. (1998). Confronting myths about teaching black children: A challenge for educators. *Teacher Education and Special Education, 21*(4), 241-254.

8. Elrich, M. (1994). The stereotype within. *Educational Leadership, 51*(8), 12-15.

9. Mendenhall, P. T. (1982). Bicultural school organization and curriculum. In R. Barnhardt (Ed.), *Cross-Cultural Issues in Alaskan Education* (Vol. II). Fairbanks: University of Alaska, Center for Cross-Cultural Studies.

Chapter 3

DISCRIMINATORY SPECIAL EDUCATION SERVICES

CULTURALLY INAPPROPRIATE EDUCATIONAL APPROACHES

History teaches that governments sometimes use education as a means of cultural or ethnic exploitation. In the past, the colonial governments that seized most of Africa and Asia and many of the missionaries that accompanied them used education to pacify and control the population, to modify the local culture, to prepare some of the locals for specific and limited kinds of work such as clerks and lower-level administrators, and so on. In South Africa under the Afrikaner regime, Black South African teachers were required to follow the racist official curriculum prepared by the Afrikaners in the schools in Black townships and homelands (1-4). While Hitler attempted to eradicate the Romani (Gypsies) in concentration camps, some eastern European countries have been trying to eradicate their culture and way of life by requiring their children to attend schools especially established for them that are designed to encourage them to adopt non-Romani ways. In Israel, although both Arabic and Hebrew are official languages and students are taught in their native language, Hebrew is a required second language in Arab language schools, but Arabic is an optional second language in Hebrew language schools. In addition, Hebrew is the language of instruction at the university level. Although the study of Jewish culture is part of the curriculum in Arabic language school, Arab culture is rarely included in Hebrew language schools (5-8).

One does not have to spend much time in schools set up by the Indonesian government in Jakarta for Dani students in Irian Jaya and the schools in the Amazon jungle and the Andes mountains set up by the Peruvian and Ecuadorian governments and religious organizations to see that teachers expend considerable effort on encouraging and requiring students to assimilate to the dominant culture's way of life. The same would apply to Norwegian schools for Lapps, the schools set up by the ruling class in Guatemala for the descendants of the Mayans, Australian schools that enroll Aboriginal students, and to many other school systems that provide disservices not services to indigenous peoples (9-10).

Schools in the United States, like in many other countries, have historically served the needs of the majority ethnic, cultural, and power group: in our case the European American middle-class majority. Once European Americans succeeded in wresting control of the territory that presently comprises the United States from the Native Americans and Hispanic Americans who shared it with them, they installed their approach to life from the Atlantic to the Pacific, Alaska, and Hawaii.

For many years, the European American way of life, including the educational system that developed to serve the needs of the upper-class and middle-class European Americans who had the power and influence to shape it, reigned supreme with no effective challenges to it. That is not to say that other cultures did not continue to survive. However, they survived in a powerless state. Most Native Americans were confined to their reservations; African Americans were subjected to stringent restrictions—first slavery and then segregation; and the Hispanic Americans who inhabited the lands taken from Mexico were considered to be inferior and treated as second-class citizens.

Over the years many events contributed to a change in the status quo. Immigration from Mexico, Puerto Rico, and other Latin American countries, China, Japan, the Philippines, and eastern Europe increased the numbers of persons who were not prepared for or able to adapt easily to the established educational system. Segregation was ended in most areas of American life, including education. The American working class unionized and gained political power. People of color gained the right to vote. With all of these developments, the demand for educational reform grew louder and louder.

One of the reformers' demands was to stop insisting that students of color act and function like European American students. This demand has not been met except in isolated cases.

Their second demand was to make education culturally relevant to all students. They insisted that school personnel should be sensitized to the importance of educationally relevant ethnic and socioeconomic-class cultural differences and the special challenges and problems poor students have to deal with because of their economic situations. They wanted educators to be trained to take such differences into consideration when planning school programs and selecting instructional, classroom management, counseling, and assessment techniques for students of color and poor students. This demand has never been met either. This is reflected in the following quotation, which summarizes the results of a national survey of the opinions of special education experts and parents of exceptional students about educational services for students of color with disabilities.

> The current educational system has a mainstream cultural bias which adversely affects the education of students from minority backgrounds. This bias is manifested in preconceived expectations about children from diverse cultures that are limiting and inaccurate. In addition, lack of awareness, sensitivity and understanding of diverse cultures by school personnel interfere with the education of students and the development of productive relationships with parents. . . . In general, the current instruction curricula, materials/methods and service delivery models are inadequate for meeting the educational needs of children from minority backgrounds. . . . Existing methods are not adequate to correctly assess/identify students from diverse backgrounds and determine appropriate educational services. Therefore, there is an over representation or under representation of students from minority backgrounds in various educational programs. (11, p. 5-7)

The opinion of these experts is supported by a great deal of research evidence (12-18).

The vast majority of special education educators who teach in ethnically diverse schools are not knowledgeable about their students' religious beliefs, values, customs, lifestyles, learning styles, behavior styles, and how the economic problems of students living in poverty affect their learning. They are unaware of the trauma many refugee students experienced prior to arriving in the United States and how it affects the way they function in school. They do not appreciate the difficulty limited English proficient students experience while trying to learn in a language they do not understand and to adjust to a strange and often-frightening school environment. In addition, they do not think that it is important to adapt their methods to the diverse needs of their students. Thus, a study found that when special education educators and regular educators were asked to prioritize the skills and competencies that teachers needed to succeed with their students, European American educators rated multicultural competencies less important than regular education competencies while African American educators rated them as more important (19).

As a result, many poor students and students of color, especially those who are immigrants, refugees, or limited English proficient are often exposed to assessment, instruction, classroom management, and counseling techniques that are appropriate for European American middle-class students with disabilities, but inappropriate for them. Having been assessed in culturally inappropriate ways, these students may have individual education plans with goals that do not fit their needs. Taught in teaching styles that do not match their culturally influenced learning styles, they may progress less rapidly than they should. When they are exposed to culturally inappropriate classroom management techniques, they are less likely to change their behavior and be accepted in mainstream classes. If they are counseled in inappropriate ways, they can have difficulty understanding, appreciating, and accepting the knowledge and advice their teachers give them.

CONTEXTUALLY INAPPROPRIATE EDUCATIONAL APPROACHES

The special educational approaches that predominate in most schools are ill suited to the living conditions of many poor students, rural students, and students of color (20-36). Immigrant and refugee students often do not receive the assistance they require to overcome the culture shock they experience on entering a new and strange environment. As a result, they may react angrily and aggressively toward teachers and systems they do not understand and cannot easily adjust to, or they may become sullen, depressed, and withdrawn. These behaviors can lead educators to refer students to programs for students with emotional and behavioral disorders.

Even when their culture shock passes, immigrant and refugee students who never attended school prior to coming to the United States because they lived in rural areas or internment camps and/or grew up in cultures that have no written languages need more help than they typically receive to learn how to learn in classes taught in foreign languages and unfamiliar teaching styles. This too can interfere with their learning and lead them to be inappropriately placed in special education programs for students with learning or developmental disabilities. Refugee students who suffer the psychological effects of the war, famine, and persecution they experienced at home or in internment camps are most likely to lack the assistance they need to overcome their problems.

Special education educators who work with refugee and immigrant students require skills in instructing students with special needs and managing the special problems they bring to school. Moreover, they need to have a high degree of tolerance for behavior that students cannot control until they have adjusted to their new educational environments.

Like foreign-born students, Native American students who live on reservations live in a region separate from mainstream America where they speak a language other than English. They too are ill prepared to adjust to and profit from a curriculum typically offered in mainstream schools that encourage beliefs and values that conflict with those of their communities and is often taught in a language they do not understand, by teachers who are unprepared to help them succeed in school. Similar to immigrant students, they too are susceptible to experiencing culture shock, identity conflicts, and feelings of alienation, confusion, and frustration.

Contextual problems make it difficult for migrant exceptional students to actualize their learning potentials. Attending school irregularly, losing considerable time traveling with their families from job to job, enrolling in numerous schools during the academic year, all contribute to their poor achievement. Lack of a stable home base, inadequate medical care, poverty, and prejudice are examples of other contextual problems that complicate their lives. Dyson has described some of the unique contextual problems migrant students must deal with.

> Imagine the problems a migrant child must face as he shifts from one school to another—perhaps as many as three times a year. Very often the migrant child does not use English as the primary language; he is not accepted readily by his classmates because he is "different"; educational approaches and textbooks tend to vary from school to school; and many times instructors are not willing to bother with a student who will be in the classroom only a few weeks. (23, p. 1)

The negative results of these problems are all too prevalent.

> Inevitably this constant interruption of learning, lack of continuity, absence from school during travel time, and often blatant discrimination by local communities and school personnel all contribute to migrant students falling behind . . . and getting disinterested in an educational system which cannot provide the needed continuous education. (21, p. 4)

These problems can be ameliorated to a considerable degree by educational programs geared to the needs of migrant students. Unfortunately, schools often add to students' problems rather than contribute to solving them.

> Migrant children with special needs are faced by a cruel double jeopardy. Special education students face serious academic difficulties even when they come from stable, affluent homes; when they are given the additional burdens of migrancy, they risk being crushed . . . . Real leadership and dedicated commitment are required if these students are to get the educations they deserve. . . The perception that they are disadvantaged makes teachers less alert to giftedness than they might be. . . . Nature puts as many geniuses among migrants as among non-migrants. . . . The opposite is worse, being larger in scale: thousands upon thousands of migrant children are diagnosed as learning impaired or mentally disabled when, in fact, their abilities are well within the normal range. . . . We must stop branding migrant children as deficient when they are merely different. (28, p. 1)

The rural communities that exceptional students call home are extremely varied. They may be living on remote islands, in rural farming areas, deserts, Arctic villages, Native American reservations, isolated mountainous regions, and so on. Economically they may come from well-off, stable farming communities, or economically depressed mining towns. Their communities may be connected to each other and to a large urban area by good roads that are open all year round; their connecting roads may be impassible during the winter, or their only means of transportation to other areas may be by plane. The special education programs rural exceptional students attend may be located in such a remote and sparsely populated area that it consists of one class that serves only a handful of students with many different disabilities and provides little in the way of additional services. It may be located close enough to a group of small towns to provide different services for students with different disabilities and a range of ancillary services, or it may be a residential facility located far from where the students' families live.

Despite these important variations, there are some important contextual factors that affect the lives and education of most rural exceptional students. In comparison to most exceptional students, rural students are twice as likely to come from poor families. They are significantly more likely to have illiterate parents, to be children of substance abusers, and victims of child abuse. They have lower self-esteem, and they have a greater tendency to be substance abusers, to experience depression, and to attempt suicide. Rural students experience many more problems and are exposed to many more adverse conditions than nonrural students.

Special education educators who work in rural areas typically face many obstacles in their attempts to assist students. Transportation difficulties to get to remote locations, vast distances between population groups, impassable roads during inclement weather, and low population density make it difficult to provide special education services to some students and prevent many families from being involved in the special education process. Although poor rural communities expend a greater percentage of their local resources on education, they are less able to afford the more costly special education services required by rural students, especially those that are required for students with low-incidence disabilities. They are also less able to afford the technological tools such as computers, interactive television, and so on that could help overcome the logistics problems mentioned earlier.

As the following description indicates, on some impoverished Native American reservations the situation for those with disabilities is especially dismal.

> Public transportation is not available on most reservations and mobility continues to be a significant problem for the disabled as well as the general population. Other services such as personal care are also rarely available, and in order to receive such services, the disabled individual who wants independence must be willing either to remain or to re-settle in an off-reservation community or urban environment. Dirt floors, substandard housing, and other inconveniences such as lack of indoor toilets make it almost impossible for many disabled people to be independent in most Indian communities. Governmental and other support for such programs have not yet reached most Indian communities. . . . Tribally operated programs also have difficulty obtaining adequate funds for their programs. Allocation of funds is not calculated on what services the disabled require or are entitled to, but are calculat-

ed based on figures or budgets for care and education of Indian children who are not disabled. (27, pp. 258, 260)

Remoteness, limited financial resources, and the unavailability of the many amenities found in urban areas make it difficult to attract and keep adequate numbers of qualified, well-trained professionals such as medical personnel and nutritionists. As a result, although rural students account for less than 30 percent of total population, the majority of unserved or underserved students with disabilities live in rural areas. In addition, too often the special educational services are provided by uncertified and poorly prepared personnel.

Estimates of the number of homeless children range from 272,773 to 1,600,000 (21, 22). The plight of homeless children and youth is especially horrendous. Many do not have their basic food, clothing, and shelter needs met. They move from place to place and shelter to shelter and attend school erratically. In comparison to those who live in homes, they have four times as many health problems and twice as many chronic diseases, but they have less access to medical care and are less able to follow the health regimes prescribed by physicians. They have more developmental delays, emotional problems, behavior disorders, and sleep disorders. They are more likely to be aggressive and noncompliant, shy and withdrawn, anxious, tired, and restless. They have greater difficulty forming relationships with others, and they are more likely to exhibit symptoms associated with stress and low self-esteem. Approximately 50 percent of them are clinically depressed, over 50 percent have contemplated suicide, and between 31 to 50 percent of them need psychiatric evaluation.

Homeless students are more likely to need special education services than students who lead more stable lives. However, the transient nature of their existence makes it difficult if not impossible for them to either comply with school systems' insistence on receiving certain documents or to be available for long periods of time while schools implement their inflexibly slow-moving special education assessment and placement processes.

The Individuals with Disabilities Education Act of 1991 (IDEA) guarantees students with disabilities the right to a free and appropriate education. The McKinney Homeless Assistance Amendments Act of 1990 encourages schools to accommodate the process they use to identify, place, and serve exceptional homeless students to the conditions in which they find themselves. However, well-intentioned laws alone have not succeeded in getting special education programs and the special education educators who work in them to adapt their approaches to the realities of homeless students' lives. Anywhere from 28 to 43 percent of them do not even attend school. According to Heflin & Rudy:

> The combination of physical, psychological, intellectual, and behavioral outcomes of homelessness for children and youth may make it difficult for them to achieve in school. Homelessness has been described as a "breeding ground" for disabling conditions. . . . Although they are clearly at risk for academic failure, the transient nature of most homeless students makes the time-consuming task of assessment and referral for special services almost impossible. Given the high percentages of homeless students experiencing school problems, child counts in special education should reflect service provision to a considerable number of learners with exceptionalities who are homeless. Analyses not only fail to document the existence of homelessness among students in special education, they also demonstrate that homeless students are often denied access to any educational opportunities. . . . A variety of legal, financial, bureaucratic, social, and familial barriers serve to effectively exclude homeless children and youth from accessing educational opportunities. (24, pp. 15-17)

LINGUISTICALLY INAPPROPRIATE EDUCATIONAL APPROACHES

In many parts of the world, governments treat problems of language diversity as a political, not an educational issue. For example, the Chinese government requires all other schools in Tibet to use Mandarin Chinese. This is not the case in the Cantonese speaking areas of China. There they can use Cantonese even though Mandarin is the official language of the country. The Chinese government also requires all schools in Tibet to follow the prescribed curriculum. As a result, less than one percent of students who begin primary school stay the course (37).

Under the Afrikaner regime, Black South African teachers were required to use Afrikans as the language of instruction in the schools in Black townships and homeland. This was true even though 93 percent of them were in favor of using English rather than "the language of the oppressor" (1-4). In Indonesia, all students are instructed in the language and dialect that is prevalent on the island of Java which is home to the politically dominant group in the country. In Ghana, because the government wants businesspeople and government officials to be proficient in English, it has decreed that all students must be taught in English after the third grade. As a result, children from poor and rural areas, who are extremely unlikely to ever need English, are taught in English despite the fact that they do not understand what they are being taught, and most of their teachers are not proficient enough in English to use it effectively as the language of instruction. Students' inability to understand English is one of the main reasons why only one percent of students who complete the sixth grade in Ghana acquire the knowledge and skills expected of them. Thus, although it is obvious that English should not be the language of instruction for most students, a political decision has been made to sacrifice these children's educational needs for the benefit of the children of the influential elite.

In a nation such as the United States that continues to be a haven for immigrants, huge numbers of students begin school without the ability to profit from instruction in English. Estimations of the number of limited English proficient students with disabilities who are not proficient enough in English to function in English-only special education programs or to be assessed using only English language assessment procedures range between 354,900 and 528,400 students (17).

The federal government through the courts and congress requires school districts to provide exceptional students with linguistically appropriate special education services. Currently however, the majority of school districts are not complying with the law. Thus, the Education of the Handicapped Act Amendments of 1990 states that:

> Services provided to limited English proficient students often do not respond primarily to the pupil's academic needs. These trends pose special challenges for special education in the referral, assessment, and instruction services for our Nation's students from non-English language backgrounds. (26)

Bilingual special education approaches (teaching students math, social studies, and other content areas in their native languages, while they are learning English as a second language) have proven to be an effective way to educate limited English proficient exceptional students (17). Unfortunately, there are too few bilingual personnel to do the job (38). Assuming that a bilingual special education educator could serve fifteen limited English proficient students and it were possible to assign students who all spoke the same language to each teacher (a very unlikely assumption) it would require between 23,000 and 35,000 bilingual special education educators to serve all limited English proficient students with disabilities. However, there are probably significantly fewer than 1,000 trained bilingual special education educators to fill at least 23,000 positions. In addition, except for a few programs that train special education educators to work with students who speak a Native American language almost all these programs focus on Spanish speaking students. Thus, students who speak any of the almost two hundred languages that are not included in these programs and students who live in areas that are not served by any of these programs cannot count on being taught by trained bilingual special education educators.

To deal with this shortage, some school districts offer bilingual special education services by teaming a monolingual special education educator with a bilingual aid who provides limited English proficient exceptional students with the additional bilingual instruction they require to learn. However, their numbers are also limited by the lack of funds to hire enough bilingual aids to serve limited English proficient students who speak many different languages.

The severe shortage of bilingual teachers and aids has led school districts to resort to other means to deal with the needs of their limited English proficient exceptional students. Some school districts avoid identifying them thereby "eliminating the problem." Some districts serve them through programs that combine English as a second language and sheltered English (39-41). In these programs, students first develop some English proficiency in an English-as-a-second-language program. Then they are taught subjects such as math, science, and social studies in a sheltered/controlled English vocabulary at their level of English comprehension while they continue to improve their English proficiency in their English-as-a-second-language classes. The available evidence suggests that when this combined approach is adapted to the special needs of students with disabilities it helps them to become proficient in English (42-44).

Training special education educators to use English-as-a-second-language and sheltered English techniques is a practical goal for special education personnel preparation programs. It does not require a bilingual professor for each of the languages spoken by students' in their service areas, nor does it require recruiting bilingual students. Nevertheless, few personnel preparation programs offer such training. Therefore, this option is not readily available to students and school districts. As Cloud has pointed out:

> Currently, a paucity of TESOL (Teachers of English to Speakers of Other Languages) programs provide cross-over training in special education, and few special education programs encourage specializations in TESOL. Professionals are left to find their own training opportunities at conferences and workshops. (39, p. 2)

The personnel shortage could be alleviated to a considerable degree if universities initiated bilingual and English-as-a-second-language special education programs. But that is not happening. School districts could assist their limited English proficient students by giving priority to bilingual teachers, aides, and psychologists when hiring new staff and by offering financial incentives for bilingual personnel. In the business world, supply and demand influences the salaries people receive. Unfortunately in public education it does not.

Prejudice against bilingual education and the resistance school districts face when they attempt to give priority to bilingual applicants restrict their ability to provide their limited English proficient students' with bilingual special education services. Many individuals are against any use of students' native languages in the classroom. Some of them erroneously believe that providing students with bilingual education endangers the preeminence of English as the language of the United States. Others are merely unaware of the effectiveness of bilingual education.

Until attitudes change, most limited English proficient exceptional students are placed in bilingual special education or English as a second language instruction. Those who are placed in regular special education programs will continue to be taught in English without regard to their linguistic needs (45, 46). Submerged in English without the skills necessary to profit from the instruction they receive, students are at risk for joining the ranks of students with disabilities who tune out their teachers, cut classes, and drop out of special education before graduating from high school.

Sometime in the mid-1980s I was hired by a school district in California to give a weeklong workshop on nonbiased assessment and instruction to selected teachers, counselors, and psychologists. The school district needed to offer the workshop because it was out of compliance with California requirements that limited English proficient students with disabilities be assessed and taught in their native languages by bilingual educators and psychologists. On the first morning of the workshop, just before I met with the forty or so people who were attending, an administrator told me something that I should have known from the get-go. Almost in passing, she gave me a "By the way I think you should know that we just adopted a policy of not hiring any new special educators, counselors, or psychologists who are not Spanish speaking. And, the non-Spanish speaking staff are threatening to sue the school district."

Well, I took a deep breath, changed my lesson plan, and walked into the room. Instead of starting the workshop as I had planned, I began by asking them to discuss the new hiring policy. Almost immediately, I discovered that the bilingual staff were sitting on one side of the room and the non-bilingual staff were on the other. I had walked into the lion's den and opened up Pandora's box.

Exceptional students also come to school speaking different dialects. People disagree about how teachers should react to them. Many educators, including many special education educators, believe that the English dialects spoken by many poor African American students (Black English/Ebonics), the dialects spoken by Native Americans, Hispanic Americans, Hawaiian Americans (Hawaiian pigeon), and certain regional dialects spoken by poor European Americans such as the ones spoken in Appalachia (mountain English) and in the greater New York City metropolitan area (New Yorkese) are inferior to standard English (the English dialect used in textbooks, newspapers, television news programs, found in grammar books, and typically used by most middle- and upper-class European Americans) and should be eradicated.

Experts however, tend to consider dialect variations to be linguistic differences rather than linguistic deficiencies (47-60). Their opinion has prevailed in the federal courts. For example, in 1979 a U.S. District Court judge ruled in favor of fifteen African American students who claimed that they were denied an equal education because their school did not take their nonstandard English dialect into account. Although this ruling affected only schools within the jurisdiction of the court, it has set a national tone. The presiding judge reflected the knowledge of the day in his ruling.

The court does not believe that language differences between "black English" and standard English to be a language barrier in and of itself.

> The unconscious but evident attitude of teachers toward the home language of the plaintiffs causes a psychological barrier to learning by the student. . . . The child who comes to school using the "Black English" system of communication and who is taught that this is wrong, loses a sense of values related to mother and close friends and siblings and may rebel at efforts by his teacher to teach reading in a different language.
> If a barrier exists because of the language used by the children in this case, it exists not because the teachers and students cannot understand each other, but because in the process of attempting to teach the students how to speak standard English the students are made somehow to feel inferior and are thereby turned off from the learning process. (61, pp. 18, 26, 36, 41-42)

Despite research findings that non-standard English dialects are not inferior forms of English, and court opinions that teachers should not discriminate against them, many special educators continue to do so (62-73). One of the ways in which special education educators and others discriminate against non-standard English speakers is to allow their judgments about students' work to be influenced by the dialect in which the students express themselves (66-73). Even when students' work is identical or of equal quality, teachers judge the oral and written work of students who speak in a Black English, or with a Hispanic, or a working-class accent to be poorer than students who speak standard English. This must cease.

A second way special education educators and others discriminate against non-standard English speakers is by evaluating them with instruments written in standard English (66-73). Poor and working-class students and students of color who speak nonstandard English dialects have difficulty demonstrating their true achievement when they are assessed in standard English. Nonstandard English speaking students may miss questions on assessment procedures that are asked using vocabulary that is not familiar to them—"behind the sofa" rather than "in back of the couch," "beginning to climb" instead of "starting to climb." They may misunderstand items because they are given in a different dialect—standard English speaking students who are asked to find which of four pictures shows "delight" typically have little difficulty identifying the picture of a girl happily eating an ice cream cone; nonstandard English speaking African American students may hear de (the) light and select the picture of a boy reading who needs a light.

For these and other reasons, teachers should never assess nonstandard English dialect speakers with standard English instruments. If they do use them with the wrong students, as a bare minimum, they should make sure students understand the directions and the items included in any assessment procedure by expressing them in the students' dialects as well as in standard English and accept answers that are correct in the students' dialects even though they may not be acceptable according to the manual.

A third way many special education educators treat nonstandard English speakers in a discriminatory manner is by correcting their nonstandard English speech and requiring them to learn to speak standard English.

They typically offer three reasons to justify their actions.

1. *Although nonstandard English dialects are not substandard, they interfere with students' academic progress.* The evidence regarding this contention is mixed. Most studies have found that speakers of nonstandard dialects do not have difficulty learning to read (56, 74-80). "One need not speak a dialect in order to understand it." (56, p. 150).

2. *Competency in oral standard English is necessary for students to learn to write standard English.* Most experts in the field agree that it is not necessary for students to be able to speak standard English to write standard English. Although nonstandard forms of English intrude in students writing when they are first learning to write standard English, the longer students remain in school the fewer

nonstandard English forms they use. That may be because writing is not speech written down.

3. *Standard English is necessary for vocational success and in other areas in which nonstandard dialect speakers are branded as uneducated and ill prepared.* Many individuals believe that community attitudes are difficult if not impossible to change quickly. They argue that schools should prepare students to succeed in the meantime. The following quotation typifies this line of thinking.

> There are many dialects in every language, but the standard form is that which is acceptable for purposes of state, business, or other everyday transactions. It is the official language of the country, and anyone who is successful in that country uses it. Those who use the nonstandard language are forever relegated to the most menial jobs and stations in life. . . . If blacks are prepared to accept the hypothesis of "black English," then they ought to be prepared to accept the relegation to "black jobs." If their preparation is second class, their lives will be second class. (60, pp. 318, 320).

It is true that many members of our society are prejudiced against certain nonstandard English dialects. However, the solution to the problem is to combat discrimination, not accommodate and acquiesce to it. Students who want to learn to speak standard English because of the advantages it offers in the biased world in which they will live and work can learn to do so. After all, it is the language of instruction in school and the medium of communication outside school.

Special education educators have an important role to play in helping non-standard English speakers. They should be correcting discrimination against non-standard English dialects and helping students deal effectively with the discrimination they experience. They should not be encouraging students to acquiesce to it. As Dean & Fowler suggested quite some time ago:

> Previously, people who have applied for a job have been judged on clothing and hair styles. These discriminations have been lessened by change of public opinion. Then, people were judged on the color of their skin or their sex. These prejudices, while still present, are being lessened with the "help" of legislation. . . . White middle-class society has reexamined its values in the previously mentioned areas of hair style, clothing, race and sex. Surely that society can have its eyes opened once again. (51, pp. 305-306)

As long as students can understand spoken and written standard English, they should be allowed or even encouraged to express themselves in their own dialects whenever they wish to do so. The following are some reasons why. Teaching students standard English before they are completely fluent in their original dialects may stunt their language development. As Kochman wrote many years ago, switching from one dialect to another "does not develop the child's ability to use language beyond what he is already capable of doing. . . . It is concerned with *how* the child says something rather than *how well* he says it" (54, p. 91).

Teachers spend too much time correcting students' dialectic vocabulary, grammatical, and pronunciation "errors." There is considerable evidence that many teachers focus on dialectical differences that are not true errors rather than concentrate their efforts on improving students' higher level skills and relate to them in productive ways.

Acceptance and appreciation of nonstandard dialects by schools and teachers improves students' self-esteem.

> Black children must be educated to learn and believe that deviation from the normative pattern of standard English is not an indication that they are abnormal. They must be helped to understand that these negative social and psychological views have resulted and can continue to result in low self-esteem, identity crisis, and self-hatred. An appreciation of Black habits, values, and goals is essential for Black children to develop a positive Black self-identity. The issue of Black English is a "good" place to start. Whites should not become reference points for how Black children are to speak and behave. (50, p. 215)

It is not possible to encourage students to learn a second dialect without also communicating that their way of speaking is less desirable. As an English teacher put it:

> No matter how carefully I explained my purpose and assured them that I was not judging their parents, grandparents, race, or culture . . . my students still resented my correcting them although most of the time they accepted my corrections in good humor. (57, p. 49)

Non-standard English speaking students and their teachers often have different perceptions of the implications of standard English. Teachers tend to view it as a way to learn more effectively and get ahead in the real world; students often view it as talking White, denying their heritage, and giving in to the European American power structure.

I felt the oppressive nature of having my way of speaking criticized in school. And, like many other kids I resisted my teachers' efforts to "help me." The junior high school that I attended in Brooklyn taught standard English. My English teachers were always correcting the way I spoke. At least it seemed that way to me. No dese, dem, and dose; no double negatives, no prepositions at the end of a sentence; don't say he don't, say he doesn't; don't say can I, say may I; don't say I will, say I shall; don't say I'll bring it wit me, say I will take it with me; don't say dem guys, say those boys; and so on. It was worse when we wrote. There were even more rules about commas, and hyphens, and preposition, and phrases, and clauses, and diagraming sentences, and so on. It seemed like my teachers didn't care what I said or wrote, only how I said and wrote it.

I never could see why the rules were so important. No one in my family or my neighborhood spoke or wrote that way. I didn't think that I should have to either. So I rebelled in junior high school and I rebelled in senior high school. At Harvard, I allowed my self to learn a little about writing standard English. But, I never learned how to use commas correctly, I continued to use contractions, and I made it a point to put prepositions anywhere I wanted to, even at the end of sentences if I felt like it.

My publications are all in standard English. But it's not my doing. Although I know that editors will add the commas where they belong, spell out contractions, and rewrite sentences so that they don't end with prepositions, I still submit my manuscripts the way I like them. And, in honor of the guys I grew up with and my New Yorkese speaking parents, grandparents, aunts and uncle, I make sure that at least a few sentences end in prepositions and a few contractions are left in.

I had another experience that brought language bias home to me. I don't know how it works now, but back in the days when I first started teaching, a New York State teaching credential wasn't good enough to teach in the New York City school system. I needed to pass the test given by the New York City Board of Education. I took the test that consisted of standing in front of an empty classroom and and teaching a lesson to an imaginary class. At the end of the lesson the examiner who was seated at the back of the room praised the content and format of my presentation; then he told me I had not passed the exam because I had a heavy Brooklyn accent. Ain't that something? Because of my accent I didn't get a license to teach kids in New York City, most of whom had even thicker accents than I had because I had been exposed to a lot of standard English speech at Harvard and had been required to take a speech class to correct my accent as part of my teacher preparation graduate program.

REFERENCES

These references describe education in South Africa under the Afrikaner regime:

1. Freer, D. (1993). The residuals of Apartheid: Impediments to teacher development in South Africa. In G. K. Verma (Ed.), *Inequality and Teacher Education: An International Perspective.* New York: Falmer Press.
2. Herman, H. D. (1992). South Africa. In P. W. Cookson Jr., A. R. Sandovnik, & S. F. Semel (Eds.), *International Handbook of Educational Reform.* New York: Greenwood.
3. Louw, W. J. (1988). Inservice upgrading of Black teachers' qualifications in South Africa. In D.K. Sharp (Ed.), *International Perspectives on Teacher Education.* Routledge: London.
4. Moodley, K. (1989). Educational ideologies and political control. In A. Yogev & S. Tomlinson (Eds.), *International Perspectives on Education and Society.* Greenwich, CT: JAI.

Inequalities in the Israeli education system are the focus of these references:

5. Adler, C. (1989). Israeli education addressing dilemmas caused by pluralism: A sociological perspective. In E. Krauz & D. Glanz (Eds.). *Education in a Comparative Context: Studies of Israeli Society* (Vol. IV), New Brunswick, NJ: Transaction.
6. Masemann, V. L. (1987). The right to education for multicultural development: Canada and Israel. In N. B. Tarrow (Ed.), *Human Rights and Education.* New York: Pergamon.

7. Mar'i, S. K. (1989). Arab education in Israel. In E. Krauz & D. Glanz (Eds.). Education in a Comparative Context: Studies of Israeli Society. Vol IV. New Brunswick, NJ: Transaction.

8. Shavit, Y. (1989). Tracking and ethnicity in Israeli secondary education. In E. Krau & D. Glanz (Eds.), *Education in a Comparative Context: Studies of Israeli Society.* (Vol. IV). New Brunswick, NJ: Transaction.

These references discuss the role of education in assimilating indigenous cultures to dominant cultures:

9. Hinckling-Hudson, A., & McMeniman, M. (1993). Beyond tokenism: Multiculturalism and teacher education in Australia. In G. K. Verma (Ed.), *Inequality and Teacher Education: An International Perspective.* New York: Falmer Press.

10. Rust, V. D. (1992). Norway. In P. W. Cookson, Jr., A. R. Sandovnik & S.F. Semel (Eds.), *International Handbook of Educational Reform.* New York: Greenwood.

This publication contains the quote about the mainstream bias of the special education system:

11. Federal Regional Resource Center. (1991). *Exploring the Education Issues of Cultural Diversity.* Lexington, KY: Interdisciplinary Human Development Institute, University of Kentucky.

The importance of providing the culturally appropriate special education services that are lacking in classrooms is detailed in the following references:

12. Ellison, C. M., Boykin, A. W., Towns, D. P., & Stokes, A. (2000). *Classroom Cultural Ecology: The Dynamics of Classroom Life in Schools Serving Low-Income African American Children.* ERIC ED 442 886.12. 13.

13. Ford, B. A. (Ed.). (1995). *Multiple Voices for Ethnically Diverse Exceptional Learners.* Reston, VA: Council for Exceptional Children.

14. Ford, B. A., Obiakor, F. E., & Patton, M. (Eds.) (1995). *Effective Education of African American Exceptional Learners: New Perspectives.* Austin, TX: Pro-Ed.

15. Garcia, S. B. (Ed.). (1994). *Addressing Cultural and Linguistic Diversity in Special Education: Issues and Trends.* Reston, VA: Council for Exceptional Children.

16. Grossman, H. (1995). *Educating Hispanic Students: Implications for Instruction, Classroom Management, Counseling, and Assessment* (2nd ed.). Springfield, IL: Charles C Thomas, Publisher, Ltd.

17. Grossman H. (1995). *Special Education in a Diverse Society.* Boston: Allyn & Bacon.

18. Serwata, T., Dove, T., & Hodges, W. (1986). Black students in special education: Issues and implications for community involvement. *Negro Educational Review, 37*(1), 17-26.

This reference reports ethnic differences in teachers evaluations of the importance of multicultural competencies:

19. Franklin, M. E., & James, J. (1997). *Are Special and General Education Teachers Likely to Provide Culturally Relevant Instruction?* Paper presented at the annual conference of the Council for Exceptional Children, New Orleans, January, 1997.

The unmet contextual problems of poor, immigrant, refugee' migrant, rural, and homeless children and adolescents with disabilities are detailed and discussed in the following references:

20. Bassuk, E. L., & Gallagher, E. M. (1990). The impact of homelessness on children. In N. A. Boxill (Ed.), *Homeless Children: The Watchers and the Waiters.* Binghamton, NY: Haworth.
21. Burns, S. (Ed.). (1991). Homelessness demographics, causes and trends. *Homewords, 3*(4), 1-3.
22. Cavazos, L. F. (1990). *U. S. Department of Education Report to Congress on the Education for Homeless Children and Youth Program for the Period October 1, 1988 through September 30, 1989.* Washington, DC: U. S. Department of Education.
23. Dyson, D. D. (1983). *Migrant Education: Utilizing Available Resources at the Local Level.* Las Cruces, NM: ERIC/CRESS.
24. Heflin, L. J., & Rudy, K. (1991). *Homeless and in Need of Special Education.* Reston, VA: Council for Exceptional Children.
25. Helge, D. (1991). *Rural, Exceptional, At Risk.* Reston, VA: Council for Exceptional Children.
26. Individuals with Disabilities Education Act (20) U. S. C., Sections 1400-1485.
27. Joe, J. R. (1988). Governmental policies and disabled people in American Indian communities. *Disability, Handicap, and Society, 3*(3), 253-262.
28. Lawless, Ken. (1986). *Neediest of the Needy: Special Education for Migrants. Harvesting the Harvesters. Book 8.* ERIC/CRESS ED 279 473.
29. Mattera, G. (1987). *Models of Effective Migrant Education Programs.* Las Cruces, NM: New Mexico State University, ERIC CRESS.
30. Matus, D. E. (1990). *Urban High School Classroom Management: A Humanistic Approach.* ERIC ED 395 049.
31. Rafferty, Y., & Rollins, N. (1990). *Homeless Children: Educational Challenges for the 1990's.* ERIC ED 325 589.
32. Reynolds, C. J., & Salend, S. J. (1990). Issues and programs in the delivery of special education services to migrant students with disabilities. *Journal of Educational Issues of Language Minority Students, 7,* 69-83.
33. Russell, S. C., & Williams, E. U. (1988). Homeless handicapped children: A special education perspective. *Children's Environments Quarterly, 5*(1), 3-7.
34. Stronge, J. H., & Tenhouse, C. (1990). *Educating Homeless Children: Issues and Answers.* Bloomington, IN: Phi Delta Kappa Educational Foundation.

35. Talbert-Johnson, C. (1998). Why so many African-American children in special education? *School Business Affairs, 64*(4), 30-35.
36. Wienke, W. D., & Miller, K. J. (1998). *Preparing General Educators to Serve Students with Learning Disabilities: Rural Classroom Applications.* ERIC ED 417 900.

The educational situations in China and Tibet are discussed this reference:

37. Postiglione, G. A. (1992). The implication of modernization for the education of China's national minorities. In R. Hayhoe (Ed.), *Education and Modernization: The Chinese Experience.* New York: Pergamon.

The effects of the shortage of bilingual special educators and psychologists are documented:

38. National Clearinghouse for Professions in Special Education, Council for Exceptional Children. Reston, VA.

The following references describe English-as-a-second-language techniques with students with disabilities and their effectiveness:

39. Cloud, N. (1988). *ESL in Special Education.* ERIC ED 303 044.
40. Cloud, N. (1990). Planning and implementing an English as a second language program. In A. L. Carrasquillo & R. E. Baecher (Eds.), *Teaching the Bilingual Special Education Student.* Norwood, NJ: Ablex.
41. Spolsky, B. (1988). Bridging the gap: A general theory of second language learning. *TESOL Quarterly, 22*, 377-396.

References that discuss sheltered English approaches and their effectiveness are listed below.

42. Chamot, A. U., & O'Malley, J. M. (1986). *A Cognitive Academic Language Learning Approach: An ESL Content-Based Curriculum.* Rosslyn, VA: National Clearinghouse for Bilingual Education.
43. Crandall, J. (Ed.). (1987). *ESL Through Content Area Instruction: Mathematics, Science, Social Studies.* Englewood Cliffs, NJ: Prentice Hall.
44. Northcutt, M., & Watson, D. (1986). *Sheltered English Teaching Handbook.* San Marcos, CA: AM Graphics & Printing.

The following references document the linguistically inappropriate special education services provided to limited English proficient students who are not placed in bilingual programs:

45. Harris, K. C., Rueda, R. S., & Supanchek, P. (1990). A descriptive study of literacy events in secondary special education programs in linguistically diverse schools. *Remedial and Special Education, 11*(4), 20-28.

46. Ortiz, A. A., & Wilkinson, C. Y. (1989). Adapting IEP's for limited English proficient students. *Academic Therapy, 24*(5), 555-568.

The following references suggest how special educators and regular educators should view and react to dialect differences:

47. Adger, C. T., Wolfram, W., Detwyler, J., & Harry, B. (1993). Confronting dialect minority issues in special education: Reactive and proactive perspectives. *Proceedings of OBEMLA Research Conference.* Washington, DC: Government Printing Office.
48. Ball, J. (1997). An ebonics based curriculum: The educational value. *Thought and Action, 13*(2), 39-50.
49. Baugh, J. (1995). The law, linguistics, and education: Educational reform for African American language minority students. *Linguistics and Education, 7*(2), 87-105.
50. Davis, B. G., & Armstrong, H. (1981). The impact of teaching Black English on self-image and achievement. *Western Journal of Black Studies, 5*(3), 208-218.
51. Dean, M. B., & Fowler, E. D. (1974). An argument for appreciation of dialect differences in the classroom. *Journal of Negro Education, 43*(3), 302-309.
52. Fields, C. D. (1997). Ebonics 101: What have we learned? *Black Issues in Higher Education, 13*(24), 18-21, 24-28.
53. Foster, H. L. (1997). *Ebonics, Standard English, and Teacher Expectations.* ERIC ED 407 687.
54. Kochman, T. (1969). *Culture and communication: Implications for Black English in the classroom.* Florida Foreign Language Reporter, Spring/Summer, 89-92, 172-174.
55. Lipscomb, D. (1978). Perspectives on dialects in Black students' writing. *Curriculum Review, 17*(3), 167-169.
56. Padak, N. D. (1981). The language and educational needs of children who speak Black English. *Reading Teacher, 35*(2), 144-151.
57. Simmons, E. A. (1991). Ain't we never gonna study no grammar? *English Journal, 80*(8), 48-55.
58. Smitherman, G., & Cunningham, S. (1997). Moving beyond resistance: Ebonics and African American youth. *Journal of Black Psychology, 23*(3), 227-232.
59. Taylor, O. L. (1986). A cultural and communicative approach to teaching standard English as a second dialect. In O. L. Taylor (Ed.), *Treatment of Communication Disorders in Culturally and Linguistically Diverse Populations.* San Diego: College-Hill Press.
60. Thomas, E. W. (1978). English as a second language—For whom? *The Crisis, 85*(9), 318-320.

Legal requirements regarding non-standard English dialects is the focus of the following reference:

61. Martin Luther King Junior Elementary School Children vs. Ann Arbor School District Board of Education, 451 F. Supplement 1324 (Michigan 1978); 463 F. Supplement 1027 (Michigan 1978); No. 7-71861, Slip Op. (Michigan, July 12, 1979).

The following references document dialect bias in teachers' evaluations of nonstandard English speaking students:

62. Elliot, S. N., & Argulewicz, E.N. (1983). The influence of student ethnicity on teachers' behavior ratings of normal and learning disabled children. *Hispanic Journal of Behavioral Sciences, 5*(3), 337-345.
63. Scheinfeld, D. R. (1983). Family relationships and school achievement among boys of lower-income urban black families. *American Journal of Orthopsychiatry, 53*(1), 127-143.
64. Taylor, J. B. (1983). Influence of speech variety on teachers' evaluation of reading comprehension. *Journal of Educational Psychology, 75*(5), 662-667.
65. Tobias, S., Cole, C., Zibrin, M., & Bodlakova, V. (1981). *Bias in the Referral of Children to Special Services.* ERIC ED 208 637.

These references describe bias resulting from assessing nonstandard dialect speakers with standard English procedures and how to avoid it:

66. Benmaman, V., & Schenck, S. J. (1986). *Language Variability: An Analysis of Language Variability and Its Influence upon Special Education Assessment.* ERIC ED 296 532.
67. Burke, S. M., Pflaum, S. W., & Knafle, J. D. (1982). The influence of Black English on diagnosis of reading in learning disabled and normal readers. *Journal of Learning Disabilities, 15*(1), 19-22.
68. Cartledge, G., Stupay, D., & Kaczala, C. (1984). *Formal Language Assessment of Handicapped and Nonhandicapped Black Children.* ERIC ED 250 348.
69. Musselwhite, C. R. (1983). Pluralistic assessment in speech-language pathology: Use of dual norms in the placement process. *Language, Speech, and Hearing Services in Schools, 14*(1), 29-37.
70. Norris, M. K., Juarez, M. J., & Perkins, M. N.(1989). Adaptation of a screening test for bilingual and bidialectal populations. *Language, Speech, and Hearing Services in Schools, 20*(4), 381-390.
71. Wartella, A. B., & Williams, D. (1982). *Speech and Language Assessment of Black and Bilingual Children.* ERIC ED 218 914.
72. Weiner, F. D., Lewnay, L., & Erway, E. (1983). Measuring language competence of Black American English. *Journal of Speech and Hearing Disorders, 48*, 76-84.

73. Williams R. L., & Rivers, L. W. (1972). *The Use of Standard Versus Non-Standard English in the Administration of Group Tests to Black Children.* Paper presented at the annual meeting of the American Psychological Association, Honolulu.

The following references shed light on the relationship between nonstandard dialects, reading, and competency in standard English:

74. Anastasiow, N. J., Levine-Hanes, M., & Hanes, M. L. (1982). *Language & Reading Strategies for Poverty Children.* Baltimore: University Park Press.
75. Bougere, M. B. (1981). Dialect and reading disabilities. *Journal of Research and Development in Education, 14*(4), 67-73.
76. Collins, J. (1988). Language and class in minority education. *Anthropology and Education Quarterly, 19*(4), 299-326.
77. Dandy, E. B. (1988). *Dialect Differences: Do They Interfere?* ERIC ED 294 240.
78. Lass, B. (1980). Improving reading skills: The relationship between the oral language of Black English speakers and their reading achievement. *Urban Education, 14*(4), 437-447.
79. Washington, V. M., & Miller-Jones, D. (1989). Teacher interaction with non-standard English speakers during reading instruction. *Contemporary Educational Psychology, 14*(3), 280-312.
80. Williams, R. L. (1997). The ebonics controversy. *Journal of Black Psychology, 23*(3), 208-214.

Chapter 4

NON-DISCRIMINATORY ASSESSMENT

The assessment approaches special education educators and other assessors use with students from many cultural, contextual, and linguistic backgrounds tend to be invalid. However, assessors can eliminate this bias by adapting their assessment procedures to these students' individual characteristics.

PREREFERRAL PROCEDURES

Bias in the assessment process begins even before students are assessed for special education placement. Teachers tend to refer poor, African American, Hispanic American, and Native American males without disabilities to programs for students with learning, emotional, behavioral, and mild cognitive disabilities. They underrefer students with gifts and talents from these backgrounds to the programs they deserve.

Students without disabilities who are not referred for assessment cannot be misplaced in programs for students with disabilities; students who are gifted and talented who are not referred for assessment cannot be placed in the programs they deserve. Therefore, it is extremely important to reduce inappropriate and biased referrals to programs for students with disabilities and to increase the number of appropriate referrals to programs for students who are gifted and talented.

Inappropriate referrals can be reduced by providing regular education teachers who have identified students who they think have learning or behavior problems that may require special education services

with assistance designed to solve the problems they observe. By helping teachers solve their problems before students are referred to special education, many inappropriate referrals can be avoided. The following steps are usually included in such a process, but not necessarily in the order indicated (1-3).

First, teachers make special efforts to help students succeed. If these
efforts prove insufficient, teachers are assisted by consultants or prob-
lem-solving teams who help them identify the reasons why students
are having difficulty and suggest culturally, contextually, and linguistically appropriate individualized instructional and classroom management techniques that regular classroom teachers can use to correct
these problems. If these modifications work, the referral process is
ended. If they do not solve the problem then and only then are students referred to be evaluated to determine whether they require special education services.

NON-DISCRIMINATORY ASSESSMENT

Adapting to Students' Cultural, Contextual, and Linguistic Characteristics

The assessment procedures used to evaluate students should suit
their cultural, contextual, and linguistic characteristics (4-13).
Otherwise the results can provide misleading and biased information.
However, while attempting to adapt their assessment procedures to
students' individual characteristics, assessors should avoid stereotyping students. Generalizations about cultural, linguistic, and contextual
differences among students can be very misleading. Students brought
up in families with similar ethnic backgrounds do not all share the
same characteristics. Parents who want their children to maintain their
own ethnic identities may pressure their children to maintain their traditional values, attitudes, and behavior patterns while parents who
wish their children to assimilate into the mainstream may do the opposite. Native American students who plan to continue to live on reservations may be less motivated to adapt to European American ways
than those who plan to leave. Poor students who identify with and
wish to join or emulate the middle class may be less likely to accept

traditional values or roles than students who are content with their economic situation.

Regional differences create diversity among ethnic and socioeconomic groups. Mexican American students who live in "border towns" in Texas, New Mexico, and Arizona, and Cuban Americans who live in areas with large Hispanic American populations such as Miami are much more likely to be exposed to the traditional Hispanic American cultural lifestyles and attitudes than Mexican American and Cuban American students who live in other parts of the United States. Likewise, students from low-income families growing up in Appalachia have somewhat different experiences and exposure to middle-class values and behavior patterns than poor students from cities such as New York, Detroit, or Atlanta.

Despite these cautions however, it is important to recognize that some descriptions of various groups of students tend to apply to the majority of their members and cut across socioeconomic-class, ethnic, geographic and other group boundaries. Such generalizations can be helpful. They can sensitize special educators to the possibility that their students may have certain attitudes, preferences, values, learning styles, and behavior patterns. However, special educators should never assume that their students will necessarily think and behave in these ways. It is as important to avoid relating to students on the basis of incorrect stereotypes as it is to avoid being insensitive to the role students' cultural, linguistic and contextual backgrounds may play in their lives. As long as special education educators keep these limitations in mind, they will be more effective with exceptional students, especially with those groups who traditionally have been overrepresented in special education, denied the services they require, or provided with special education services that do not meet their needs. The following are some students' characteristics that assessors should consider when evaluating students.

Students come to the assessment process with different test-taking skills. Students who have not acquired test-taking skills such as when to ask the assessor for clarification or assistance, when to work fast, when to guess and to skip difficult items, how to rule out items in multiple choice items that are obviously meant to mislead or entrap students, and so on may be unable to demonstrate what they actually know and can do. Improving students' test-taking skills, including those of African American, Hispanic American, Native American, and poor students, improves their scores on assessment procedures and reduces their misplacement in special education (4, 10).

Students are not equally motivated to do their best when they are assessed. Some students may not realize that the assessment being conducted is designed to evaluate them. As a result, they do not try to do as well as they might if they understood the significance of the situation (7). Some students of color, particularly African American and Hispanic American males, are motivated to avoid success in school so as not to appear to their peers to be "acting White" (10, 14-21). Students who are not motivated to succeed in school may be equally unmotivated to perform their best on school-related assessments. Therefore, to make sure that such students demonstrate what they have learned and can do, assessors may have to motivate them to do their best. When they do not do so or their attempts fail, assessors should take students' lack of test-taking skills and motivation into consideration when they interpret and report the results they obtain.

When attempting to motivate students to do their best, assessors can adapt their techniques to students' motivational styles. For example, students who are brought up to view their family as their main reference point when evaluating themselves are likely to respond positively to statements such as if they do their best during the assessment their family will be proud of them and it will reflect positively on their families and communities.

It is also helpful to know whether individual recognition or anonymity is stressed in students' cultures. Many Hispanic American students and some European American females who have difficulty with public recognition are more likely to try their best when they are assured that their anonymity will be preserved, not when they anticipate that their achievement will be recognized publicly.

Whether students prefer competitive or cooperative situations is also important. Chamberlain and Medinos-Landurand point out that,

> In American society, students who do not value or are not skilled in competition are at a serious disadvantage in the testing process. These students do not understand or accept the concept of doing their "best" and working to do better than others during a test. (5, p. 118)

Hispanics, Hawaiian Americans, and Native Americans, among others however, tend to prefer cooperative environments and may respond better to cooperative motivating techniques during the assessment process.

Some noncompetitive students may do whatever necessary to avoid appearing to be competitive with other individuals. Although it is difficult for many European American teachers to believe, some Hispanic Americans and Native Americans may pretend that they do not know the answer to a question or a problem if one of their peers has not given the right answer.

> Calling upon a boy or girl to correct an answer or to supply information in response to a question missed by someone else, creates a problem situation for, in the Latino code of ethics, it is not considered proper for any individual to secure attention at the expense of another person (showing up his ignorance, for instance). (6, p. 78)
>
> If a question is asked and one child cannot answer it, no one else (American Indian student) will because that means they would have placed themselves in a superior position over their peer. (12, p. 135)

Some students become anxious when they are assessed. A small amount of anxiety can motivate students to do their best when they are assessed; however, too much anxiety can interfere with their performance. Immigrant and refugee students who have never been assessed are likely to be anxious during the assessment process. African American, Hispanic American, and poor students tend to become anxious when they are evaluated by individuals who are not from their backgrounds (9, 10).

> Black children are taught early to be suspicious of whites. . . . Thus Blacks grow up believing that whites cannot be trusted. Whether this is true or not is hardly the question, for we are dealing here with perceptual realities of Blacks. . . . The effect of such an attitude on any testing situation in which the instrument is administered by a white is obvious. . . . From an intercultural point of view the testing situation is even more complicated. The situation itself, in all probability is defined as being cold in the negative sense of that Black term. Black Americans looking at Euro-American interactional style often brand whites as cold and aloof. This feeling about whites will then be intensified if the situation is kept under the control of the tester. Not only does this environment ignore the means by which significant information is generally passed on among Blacks . . . but it eliminates the possibility of establishing the kind of relationship that makes anything but hostile responses seem appropriate to the testee.

> In this sense it is not the questions per se which cause Black children difficulty, it is the testing environment in general and especially the techniques that are used to ask the questions. (8, pp. 338-339)

Assessors should do what they can to relieve students' anxiety and suspicions. If they do not succeed, they should not begin or continue the evaluation and invalidate any results they have obtained up to that point.

Students' communication styles influence the results of their assessments. Some students expect others to be sensitive enough to their feelings and problems that it is unnecessary for them to be open and direct about their needs. If they have to do so, they may experience a loss of self-respect and think that others have also lost respect for them as well (10).

> Because Hispanics tend to feel that it reflects negatively on their self-worth to admit that they do not know something or cannot do something, Hispanic students who are less accustomed to asking questions and expressing doubts and confusions may not admit that they do not understand directions or items included in assessment procedures. (9, p. 195)

Therefore assessors should not assume that students who do not ask for help in understanding directions and so on are really ready to perform the required assessment task.

Children are brought up to be more or less loquacious with adults. In comparison to European American students, Native American, Asian and Pacific Island American, and Hispanic American students typically are expected to talk less and listen more when they converse with adults. Thus, they may respond in as few words as possible during assessment procedures and be penalized for not saying enough or providing enough details.

Students' learning styles can also influence the way they function when they are assessed. No children are brought up to be completely dependent on or independent of adults. However, some youngsters are trained to accomplish things on their own; others, for example Hispanic Americans, are brought up to be more dependent on the aid, support, opinions, and feedback of their parents and other significant adults. Standardized assessment procedures that do not permit assessors to provide learners with the supportive environment they require to demonstrate their accomplishments tend to underestimate these learners' accomplishments or potentials. Therefore it is important to know whether students are prepared to be relatively self-reliant and independent during the assessment process, or require a great deal of guidance and feedback to perform at their optimum level.

Some students, particularly, Hispanic Americans and Native Americans, are unlikely to choose an answer they are not completely sure of on a multiple choice item. As a result they may not follow advice to guess at answers they are not sure of.

> A reluctance to try too soon and the accompanying fear of being "shamed" if one does not succeed may account for the seemingly passive uninterested and unresponsive attitude of Indian students. (11, p. 28)
>
> The Hispanic culture discourages guessing (hablando sin saber). Thus, Hispanic students may be penalized on assessment procedures which require students to respond when they are uncertain of the correct answer. (9, p. 195)

Students differ in terms of their tolerance for and willingness to continue to perform assessment tasks that are boring, monotonous, tedious, and repetitious. African American students who come from homes that are highly stimulating tend to do better when the format of an assessment procedure includes more task variation, but the performance of African American and European American students from homes that are not highly stimulating does not improve with increased variability.

Students' willingness to sit still for long periods of time is greatly influenced by their ethnic and socioeconomic-class backgrounds. Because some students may have difficulty sitting quietly and completing sedentary assessment activities for long periods of time, their poor performance may indicate their difficulty adjusting to the requirements of the assessment situation and not what they have achieved or learned.

People from different cultures work and play at different paces. Because of their upbringing, some students attempt to accomplish as much as possible within a given period of time; others prefer a relaxed steady pace. African Americans, Hawaiian Americans, Hispanic Americans, Filipino Americans, and many other groups of students of color who tend to work at slower paces cannot always show on timed procedures what they can do or have learned. Two students may both obtain a score of 30 on a fifty-item test that is equal to a sixth-grade math level or a 73 percentile rank on an achievement test. However if one of them, a fast-working student, finished the test and only knew the answer to thirty questions and the second one, a slower-working student, only had time to answer the first thirty questions, their math abilities are very different. Moreover, students who are accustomed to working at a slower pace may make more errors when required to work as fast as they can whereas students accustomed to a faster pace, for example, Japanese Americans and Chinese Americans, continue to perform as well when they are told to work as fast as they can (10).

Students require different amounts of time to prepare their answers when called on in class or asked to respond to a question during the assessment process. Shade describes the difference as follows:

> Some people are rather anxious to insure that they gather all the information possible before being asked to respond and they have a need to be accurate. These individuals are considered to be *reflective* while those individuals who respond immediately to what is presented without regard to the fact they may be erroneous are labeled as *impulsive* learners. (13, p. 17)

Native American students tend to look at all sides of an issue, examine their possible implications, and make sure they know the answer before they are ready to express their opinion. Timed tests penalize them. Teachers who do not allow them sufficient time to prepare their answers before calling on someone else or moving on to the next item may mistakenly believe that they do not know something, are slow learners, and so on.

For these reasons, it is essential to use untimed procedures whenever possible and to make sure that students are not recommended for placement in special education or denied admission to programs for students with gifts and talents based on the results of evaluation procedures that are culturally inappropriate because they are timed.

Non-biased Assessment Materials and Procedures

The materials and procedures that assessors use are another significant source of bias. For example, the items on intelligence tests are supposed to measure students' ability to learn and to assist assessors to predict how students will learn when they are given certain kinds and amounts of assistance. Students' current knowledge about a particular item such as how far is it from one place to another, the height of the average American adult male, or their ability to perform a particular task like forming a design from blocks might conceivably indicate their learning potential or help assessors to predict how they will learn in the future, but only under certain conditions. The students must have been exposed to the information or task and have had sufficient practice to learn it. They must be motivated to demonstrate their knowledge or ability to assessors. They have to be permitted to do so in a way that fits their performance style.

Students of color, poor, and limited English proficient students are not always exposed to the same materials, tasks, environments, and so on as European American, middle-class, and English proficient students. A question such as how far is it from one place to another is only relevant if students are familiar with the places. Asking why it is better to pay bills by check rather than cash is not relevant to children whose parents cannot afford a checking account. The answers to such items as what should you do if a smaller child hits you, why is it better to give money to a charitable organization than to a street beggar, and what should you do if you lose something that belongs to your friend depend on the values and experiences students have been exposed to.

Different teachers, schools, and school districts include different content in the courses they offer at each grade level. Inner-city schools, rural schools, and suburban schools include very different skills in their curriculum. Migrant students who move from school to school may miss a considerable amount of course content. For these reasons, assessment procedures may evaluate students on what they should have been taught, not on what they were actually taught.

One way to reduce such bias is to eliminate any items that are more difficult for some groups than for others. Although test developers discard items that are more difficult for one gender or the other to eliminate gender bias, they do not do the same thing for items that are more difficult for students of color and poor and working-class students.

As noted previously, many students may not be motivated to demonstrate their ability and knowledge to strangers during the assessment procedure. Students may not be able to show what they know and can do if there is a poor match between the ways they function and the format of an assessment procedure—the way tasks, questions, and so on are posed to students and the way in which students are required to respond to them.

Students who are immigrants or who have attended atypical schools on reservations may have difficulty adjusting to the unfamiliar format of many standardized tests. For example, some assessment procedures require students to fail five, six, or even seven similar items before they can go on to the next group of items. This can be devastating to students who are not accustomed to taking tests in which they fail many items and still do well.

Assessment materials that can be used with students who function at many different levels often contain both very easy and very difficult problems on the same page. This can be very frightening and demoralizing to students who see many problems or items that are too difficult for them and do not understand that the the difficult ones are for students who are older or in a higher grade than they are.

As noted earlier, some students, especially African Americans, Hispanic Americans and Native Americans, cannot always show what they can do on timed procedures. Providing these students with the time they need to complete an assessment at the pace at which they are accustomed to work, provides more accurate information about what they know and can do.

Assessments conducted in a language or dialect in which students are not proficient or in only one language when students require two languages to function adequately and explain themselves fully do not provide a true picture of what students know or can do (22, 23). Students who have no proficiency in English clearly need to be assessed in their native language. Those that are truly proficient in English can be assessed completely in English. However, many limited English proficient students have two vocabularies—a home vocabulary and a school vocabulary—and need to be assessed in two languages to demonstrate what they know and can do.

The goal of providing students with linguistically appropriate assessment services in the more than one hundred languages spoken by limited English proficient students in the United States has proved difficult to achieve (10). Very few of the regular education educators, special education educators, and psychologists who are responsible for assessing students for possible placement in special education programs are bilingual. This is especially true for languages other than Spanish. In addition, except for Spanish language materials, there is very little assessment material in the many languages spoken by the millions of limited English proficient students in the public schools.

The two approaches that have been used to overcome these difficulties, translating assessment materials into other languages and using interpreters during the assessment process, are problematic.

Translating materials into students' native languages can improve the performance of limited English proficient students. However, there are a number of problems that must be avoided before these benefits can be achieved. Poorly translated materials will not improve the validity of an assessment. A translated word may have more than one meaning. For example, translating the English word "courage" into the Spanish word "valor" becomes problematic because valor means value as well as bravery in Spanish. Translating material often changes in level of difficulty of items. "Dog," a very easy word to read or spell in English translates to "perro" in Spanish, a more difficult word because of double "rr." Translating "building" to "edificio" makes the item easier.

Translating material into English will not necessarily eliminate its content bias. Therefore, it is often necessary to adapt the contents as well as the language of the material to the cultural, contextual, and linguistic characteristics of the students with whom they are to be used. Actual examples of content change in translations include changing the question "How are a peach and a plum ?" to "How are an orange and a banana alike?" replacing a marble game with a card game, and modifying "How far is it from New York to Chicago?" to "how far is it from New York to Puerto Rico?"

Sometimes it is necessary to accept alternative correct answers to some items. For example, what is absurd about a picture of man carrying an umbrella upside down to middle-class European American children is that the umbrella is in a position that it will not protect him from rain. However, to Puerto Rican children the absurdity is that a man is carrying an umbrella in any position because males do not carry umbrellas.

The assistance of interpreters is a must when assessors cannot evaluate limited English proficient students and interview their parents in their native language. When properly used, interpreters can be very helpful. The use of untrained or poorly prepared interpreters, however, can create many problems. Untrained interpreters who identify with the students and want the students to do well rather than demonstrate their true abilities and disabilities may prompt the right answer from the student or modify their answers so that they are closer to the acceptable response. Interpreters who are not equally fluent in both languages may translate incorrectly to the student or assessor. Interpreters who are fluent in students' languages but not knowledgeable about their cultural background may translate correctly but conduct the assessment in a culturally inappropriate manner or fail to notice content and format bias. If interpreters are from a different socioeconomic-class, religious, racial, or ethnic background than the students, they may be prejudiced against them.

To avoid or at least minimize these potential problems interpreters should be trained in the principles of assessment, human development, special education, and so on. They should be equally competent in both languages, equally familiar with the mainstream American culture and students' cultures, and if possible, familiar with the communities in which students live and the subgroups to which they belong.

As noted earlier, nonstandard dialect-speaking students who are poor, African American, Native American, Hispanic American, or from Appalachian areas also perform poorly when they are assessed in standard English. Therefore, special education educators should never assess nonstandard English dialect speakers with standard English instruments.

Informal Assessment

Assessment procedures can be standardized or informal. Standardized procedures are administered and scored in a uniform way. The interpretation of the scores is typically accomplished by comparing an individual's score to norms obtained from a sample of students that are believed to represent the population of students with whom the procedure will be used. The results of a standardized procedure might indicate that a student is functioning at the fourth grade in vocabulary (because her scores on the test were the same as the average of fourth graders in the norm sample) or that she is in the top 10 percent of fourth graders (because her scores on the vocabulary test were higher than 90 percent of the fourth graders in the norm sample).

Informal procedures typically involve evaluating what students do, how they function, and what they have learned in relation to the curriculum they are exposed to or the goals of their particular teacher or school. This can be done in an unstructured manner by observing how students function and evaluating their work or in a structured way by using observation checklists, scales, and lists of specific evaluative criteria. The results of an informal, nonstandardized procedure might indicate that a student has learned 85 percent of the vocabulary words that a teacher assigned the class.

Educators have always used informal approaches to assess students. The typical weekly spelling, math, and social studies tests are examples of informal approaches to assessing students' academic progress. Deciding whether a student who is a refugee has emotional problems or merely conforming to a cultural pattern by comparing his behavior to that of other students who have a similar background is an example of informal assessment of students' behavior. Asking a student's parents to compare her adaptive behavior at home and in the community with those of her siblings, cousins, or other neighborhood children is an informal way of evaluating a student's out-of-school achievement.

Educators and other concerned persons have been criticizing the standardized tests used in regular and special education with poor students, and students of color since the early 1920s (2, 24-26). However, these criticisms did not receive a great deal of attention from special educators and psychologists until 1968 when the Association of Black Psychologists, a subgroup of the American Psychological Association, called for a moratorium on the standardized testing of African American students. The association criticized achievement, intelligence, aptitude and performance tests because they were being used to:

1. label black people as uneducable
2. place black children in special education
3. perpetuate inferior education
4. assign black children to lower educational tracks
5. deny black children higher educational opportunities
6. destroy positive intellectual growth and development of black people (25, pp. 17-18).

A spokesperson for the Association claimed that,

Classification systems based upon standardized tests have systematically labeled a disproportionately large number of minority group children as abnormal, intellectually subnormal and a disproportionately small number of minority group children as normal and gifted...

1. Children who are misclassified and labeled as "different" may be permanently stigmatized and may experience rejection by those in their immediate environment.
2. They may be assigned to inferior educational programs or deprived of their freedom through commitment to an institution.
3. They may be excluded from opportunities which are vital for the full development of their emotional and physical existences.
4. They may be committed to institutions, which define and confirm them as delinquent, retarded or emotionally disturbed. Thus, the child will manifest behaviors which are appropriate to his label. They become more inclined to crime, more disturbed than they would be under more normal growth conditions and less bright than they could be. (26, pp. 3-4, 8-9)

Other criticisms of standardized assessment have included:

- They do not accurately/validly describe how students function in the present nor predict how students will function in the future.
- They ask "Do you know what I the test developer think you should know" rather than "What do you know."
- They are not easily adapted to students' contextual, cultural, and linguistic characteristics.
- The data obtained with standardized instruments are often collected in non-classroom situations under unusual circumstances by unfamiliar assessors and therefore do not reflect how students function in real-life classrooms with real-life teachers.
- Percentile ranking, grade-level placements, and other norms provided by standardized tests are not realistic because national norms are not necessarily true for a given school district, school, or class. The contents of courses taught at seventh-grade level in a predominantly middle-class suburban school may be very different from the course contents in a school serving predominantly poor urban students. Thus, students who score at seventh-grade level on nationally normed reading tests may actually be functioning much lower than the typical seventh-grade student in a middle-class neighborhood suburban school and much higher than the typical seventh-grade student in some other school districts.
- They require all students to fit a preconceived mold.

> Despite the lip-service we pay to the myriad ways in which individuals differ, and claim to celebrate this variety, our practices speak otherwise. In fact

it is performance on these tests–with their narrow and rigid definition both of when children should be able to perform particular skills and how they should be able to exhibit their knowledge–that determines whether we see children as "okay" or not. In the process we damage all children–we devalue the variety of strength they bring with them to school. All differences become handicaps. (24, p. 47)

- Standardized procedures make it difficult for assessors to determine the reasons why students obtain their scores. Unless they examine students' answers carefully and/or interview them they cannot tell from students' scores alone if students were familiar with the procedure, if they lacked sufficient time to complete the procedure, whether they did not ask questions when they did not understand the directions, whether they would not guess when guessing was to their advantage, whether they were not motivated to perform their best, and so on.

Informal assessments can have many advantages over standardized assessments. The information they provide has a more direct relationship to the decisions teachers have to make about instructing and managing students, for example, what their strengths and weaknesses are, what skills they have and have not acquired, and more. They evaluate students in terms of activities, skills, and subject matter that they have actually been taught and practiced. They can be used to determine if students have accomplished the goals set by the teacher, department, or school district.

However, informal assessments can be used in a discriminatory manner. Assessors who are biased against students of color and poor students may give vent to their biases when they evaluate students informally. Those who are are not prejudiced may mistakenly interpret what they observe from their own cultural, contextual, and gender point of view. As Hilliard pointed out many years ago:

A given style user will take the behavior of another style user and will not experience it as that behavior actually is, but will reinterpret that experience in terms of her own experiential views or her own experiential framework, thus frequently losing the essence of the experience of the person being observed. In some cases the assessor can comprehend the experiences of another style user only by actually "changing" that person's experience. (27, p. 44)

To avoid such bias, informal and formal assessment results should be reported along with a description of the context in which they were obtained and any limitations due to the assessors' lack of knowledge or experience. This should include such contextual factors as students' familiarity with the material and format of procedure, whether they were anxious or tense while they were being assessed, their motivation to perform well, whether they completed all parts and items of the procedure or were limited by time constraints, their reaction to assessor, possible linguistic problems, and so on. Assessor limitations might include lack of fluency in the language spoken by students, inability to interpret the results obtained in terms of students' experiences, possible assessor bias, and so on.

There are a number of well-thought-out and organized informal nonstandardized approaches that can be superior to standardized assessment. Three approaches—portfolio assessment, curriculum-based assessment, and test-teach-test approaches—are particularly useful (10).

Portfolio assessment, also called assessment in context, situational testing, and authentic assessment emphasizes assessing what students actually do or perform. Portfolios contain evidence of students' work that tells the story of their accomplishment and process of achieving it. The material in a portfolio can be constructed, created, or described by students: material that is audiotaped, written, videotaped, or photographed. Portfolios can contain only students' final, completed work or their work at different stages over time showing how their work improved. They may include a number of totally different tasks or the same task performed many times over the course of weeks, months, a semester, or a year. They may also contain students' grades, test scores, honors, testimonies from others, teachers' observation and evaluation of students' performance, interview protocols, student self-reports, and so on.

Portfolio assessment evaluates students in terms of real-life authentic tasks in the situations in which students are actually functioning. It provides much more detailed and comprehensive data than an answer on a multiple choice item. It enables students' to use their preferred learning and communication styles and linguistic ability in English and their native language to demonstrate their accomplishments.

However, because teachers' evaluations of poor students and students of color can be prejudiced, the use of subjective portfolio assessment may lead to even more bias than results from objective standardized procedures.

Curriculum-based assessment evaluates students in terms of the curriculum they have and are studying. To use a curriculum-based evaluation approach, a school district or a similar entity establishes the contents and objectives of a particular curriculum such as fifth-grade math, third-grade spelling, American History 2, or Spanish 3 and develops a series of probes—assessments that teachers and others can employ to determine how well students have achieved each of these objectives. Examples of typical probes include the number of words students read correctly in a reader or word list and the number of words spelled correctly from a spelling list.

These probes can be used to compare students' achievement of the objectives of the curriculum to their peers' achievement on the same curriculum. This enables assessors to determine if students are far enough behind to warrant possible referral to or enrollment in special education. By evaluating students' achievement in many areas of the curriculum—reading, spelling, written language, and math computation—educators can obtain an estimate of their overall ability. They can then compare this estimate to students' achievement in a particular subject area to determine whether it is significantly below their general potential to qualify them for programs for students with learning disabilities. Curriculum-based assessment can also be used to monitor students' progress in the curriculum, to determine whether students have achieved a particular goal, and whether they have progressed to the point that they no longer require special education services.

Curriculum-based assessment offers some advantages over standardized tests. It avoids the problem of assessing students on tasks, skills, and knowledge that they have not been taught. It does not compare students to norms based on a national sample of students many of whom attend schools that do not resemble theirs and live in other parts of the country. Because it can be administered informally as part of the regular classroom activities, it may make students less anxious and thereby provide a more accurate measure of their achievement. It is more sensitive to short-term improvement in student achievement and provides information that can be used to make day-to-day instructional decisions.

Curriculum-based assessment approaches can be used to differentiate low-achieving students from students with learning disabilities. Its use during the prereferral phase has reduced the number of students who are eventually assessed and the proportion of referred students found to require special education programs (10).

The test-teach-test approach, also called assisted assessment, reciprocal teaching, and dynamic assessment is an assessment method that is designed to evaluate students' learning potential by studying how they actually learn. As its name implies, the test-teach-test approach includes three steps. First, students' achievement or functioning is assessed. Then assessors attempt to remediate or improve the students' functioning or achievement. Last, students' are reevaluated to determine the extent of improvement that can be expected as well as how much and what kinds of additional help are required for a given amount/degree of improvement.

Most standardized intelligence tests are based on the assumption that students' learning potentials are reflected in what they have learned. They measure what students know and can do and attribute more learning potential to students who know more of the information and can do more of the tasks included in the assessment procedure. The test-teach-test method, on the other hand, provides a direct measure of the extent to which students can learn if given additional help. It also reveals how much and what kinds of additional help students' require to reach a specific goal or standard. It focuses on the trainability or educability of students' cognitive processes (learning abilities).

The test-teach-test approach can produce biased data if assessors are not sufficiently knowledgeable about students to adapt the instructional techniques they use in the teach phase of the approach to students' cultural, contextual, gender, and linguistic characteristics. When assessors use inappropriate instructional techniques they may incorrectly attribute the students' limited improvement to their "limited learning potential" rather than to the assessors' inappropriate teaching techniques. Despite these potential problems, the test-teach-test approach has proven useful with many students including students of color (28, 29).

Gender-Appropriate Assessment

One of the reasons why boys are overrepresented in special education classes for students with behavioral and learning problems and attention deficit, hyperactivity disorders is that teachers are intolerant of male-typical behavior patterns (30-48). In comparison to girls, boys tend to be more active, more noisy, and less calm. That may be the reason why teachers often mislabel males who exhibit a higher level of active behavior than they find acceptable as hyperactive. In fact, males who have been identified as having attention deficit hyperactivity disorder outnumber females by between 4 to 1 and 10 to 1 depending on the study.

Boys are less polite, less helpful, and appear to be more aggressive and assertive than girls because their aggressive behavior which is physical—pushing, shoving, hitting and so on—is more obvious to teachers than females' relational aggression—ostracizing others from the group, telling stories about them, saying nasty things about them, and so on. Male-type aggressive behavior bothers most teachers more than the relational aggression that characterizes females.

Because of their bias against male-typical aggressive and assertive behavior, teachers are more likely to notice when boys behave aggressively, and they are more likely to react to it. As a result, aggressive boys are more likely to get into trouble than aggressive girls.

Girls are also more likely to experience themselves as sad or depressed than boys, who are angry more often than girls. Sad or depressed students tend to be quiet. However, angry students who show their emotions in angry outbursts can be quite disruptive, especially if they are boys who continue to express their feelings more intensely. Therefore, although girls have at least as many emotional problems as boys, because they tend to not act out when they are emotional, teachers are more likely to notice boys with emotional problems and refer them to special education programs for students with emotional problems.

Boys tend to deal with conflicts openly and are more likely to settle arguments by fighting. Females generally tend to avoid conflicts with others, rather than deal with them openly which is the approach teachers prefer. In their relations with teachers, boys are less willing to conform to their expectations to obtain their approval, which is a definite problem for them. These gender differences may help explain why so many more boys than girls are referred to programs for students with behavioral disorders.

Avoiding overreferring boys to these programs teachers will have to become more tolerant of male-typical behavior patterns and learn to deal with such behavior without pushing boys out of their classes and into special education programs. Assessors will have to distinguish between behavior that reflects male-typical patterns and behavior

---

Like many teachers, I too had gender biases when I started teaching. I was certainly less tolerant of my male students' behavior problems than those of my female students. My first job was teaching emotionally disturbed and delinquent teenagers in single-sex classes. Because the classes were small and I was teaching the same classes twice, I came up with the idea of combining them. My supervisors were worried about control issues; I was raring to go. So we did it.

Some of the students who had been in the single-sex classes changed their behavior patterns. A few well-behaved students, primarily, but not exclusively males, assumed a more delinquent demeanor. They began to challenge me, made jokes that indicated to the others that they really didn't buy everything I was selling, and so on. A few of the girls became shy and stopped volunteering answers or participating in class discussions. Looking back at how I responded to these changes, the increase in delinquent behavior galvanized me into action, but I hardly noticed or reacted to the girls' withdrawal.

---

caused by emotional and behavioral problems.

REFERENCES

These references discuss the prereferral process:

1. Markowitz, J., Garcia, S. B., & Eichelberger, J. H. (1997). *Addressing the Disproportionate Representation of Students from Racial and Ethnic Minority Groups in Special Education: A Resource Document.* ERIC ED 406 810.
2. Murdick, N. L., & Petch-Hogan, B. (1996). Inclusive classroom management: Using preintervention strategies. *Intervention in School and Clinic, 31*(3).

3. Reschly, D. J. (1997). *Disproportionate Minority Representation in General and Special Education: Patterns, Issues, and Answers.* ERIC ED 415 632.

Student characteristics that assessors should consider when they evaluate students are described in these publications:

4. Bell-Mick, L. (1983). *Assessment Procedures and Enrollment Patterns of Cuban-Americans, Mexican-Americans, and Puerto Ricans in Special Education Programs.* Paper presented at the annual meeting of the American Educational Research Association, Montreal.

5. Chamberlain, K.P., & Medinos-Landurand, P. (1991). Practical considerations for the assessment of LEP students with special needs. In E. V. Hamayan & J. S. Damico (Eds.), *Limiting Bias in the Assessment of Bilingual Students.* Austin, TX: Pro-ED.

6. Condon, E. C., Peters, J. Y., & Sueiro-Ross, C. (1979). *Special Education and the Hispanic Child: Cultural Perspectives.* Philadelphia: Temple University, Teacher Corps Mid-Atlantic Network.

7. Deyhle D. (1987). Learning failure: Tests as gatekeepers and the culturally different child. In H. E. Trueba (Ed.), *Success or Failure?* Rawley, MA: Newbury House.

8. Gay, G., & Abrahams, R. D. (1973). Does the pot melt, boil, or brew? Black children and white assessment procedures. *Journal of School Psychology, 11*(4), 330-340.

9. Grossman, H. (1995). *Educating Hispanic Students: Implications for Instruction, Classroom Management, Counseling,and Assessment* (2nd ed.) Springfield, IL: Charles C Thomas Publishers, Ltd.

10. Grossman, H. (1995). *Special Education in a Diverse Society.* Boston: Allyn & Bacon.

11. Longstreet, E. (1978). *Aspects of Ethnicity.* New York: Teachers College Press.

12. Lyons, G. (1979). A high school on an Indian reservation: A question of survival, developing goals, and giving leadership. *British Educational Administration Society, 7,* 130-138.

13. Shade, B. J. (1979). *Racial Preference in Psychological Differentiation: An Alternative Explanation for Group Differences.* ERIC ED 179 672.

These references discuss "acting white":

14. American Broadcasting Corporation, *20/20.* (June 7, 1999). *"Acting White."*

15. Bergin, D. A., & Cooks, H. C. (1995). *"Acting White": Views of High School Students in a Scholarship Incentive Program.* ERIC ED 385 632.

16. Collins-Eaglin, J., & Karabenick, S. A. (1993). *Devaluing of Academic Success by African-American Students: On "Acting White" and Selling Out."* ERIC ED 362 587.

17. Fordham, S., & Ogbu, J. U. (1986). Black students' school success: Coping with

the burden of "acting white." *Urban Review, 18*(3), 176-206.

18. Jenks, C., & Phillips, M. (1998). *The Black-White Test Score Gap.* Washington, DC: Brookings Institution Press.

19. Kusimo, P. S. (1999). *Rural African Americans and Education: The Legacy of the Brown Decision. ERIC Digest.* ERIC ED 425 050.

20. Romo, H. (1997). *Improving Ethnic and Racial Relations in the Schools. ERIC Digest.* ERIC ED 414 113.

21. Sylvester, P. S. (1994). Elementary school curricula and urban transformation. *Harvard Educational Review, 64*(3), 309-331.

These references discuss the biased assessment of limited English proficient students:

22. Assaf-Keller, M. (1990). *Bilingual Learning Disabilities Services in Illinois—A Myth?: A Look at Policy.* ERIC ED 329 094.

23. Figueroa, R. A., & Hernandez, S. (2000). *Testing Hispanic Students in the United States: Technical and Policy Issues.* ERIC ED 441 652.

Criticisms of the use of standardized tests with students of color can be found in these references:

24. Howe, H., & Edelman, M. (1985). *Barriers to Excellence: Our Children at Risk.* Boston: National Coalition of Advocates for Students.

25. Williams, R. L. (1974). A history of the Association of Black Psychologists: Early formation and development. *Journal of Black Psychology, 1*(1), 9-24.

26. Williams, R. L. (Guest Editor). (1975). *Testing of the Afro-American. Journal of Afro-American Issues, 3.* As quoted in R. L. Williams & H. Mitchell, *Whatever Happened to ABPSI's Moratorium on Testing: A 1968-1977 Reminder.* St. Louis: Washington University.

Assessor bias that can occur in informal assessment is discussed in this reference:

27. Hilliard III, A. G. (1976). *Alternatives to IQ testing: An Approach to the Identification of Gifted "Minority" Children.* ERIC ED 148 038.

These references discuss the use of the test-teach-test method with students of color:

28. Hilliard III., A. G. (1992). The pitfalls and promises of special education practice. *Exceptional Children, 59*(2), 168-72.

29. Pena, E., Quinn, R., & Iglesias, A. (1992). The application of dynamic meth-

ods to language assessment: A nonbiased procedure. *Journal of Special Education, 26*(3), 269-280.

These references discuss gender differences and how they can affect the assessment process:

30. Buntaine, R. L., & Costenbader, V. K. (1997). Self-reported differences in the experience and expression of anger between girls and boys. *Sex Roles: A Journal of Research, 36*(9-10), 625-637.
31. Campbell, J., & Frabutt, J. M. (1999). *Familial Antecedents of Children's Overt and Relational Aggression.* ERIC ED 430 705.
32. Carlo, G., Raffaelli, M., & Meyer, K. A. (1999). Why are girls less physically less aggressive than boys?: Personality and parenting mediators of physical aggression. *Sex Roles: A Journal of Research, 40*(9), 711-729.
33. Crick, N. R., Casas, I. F., & Mosher, M. (1997). Relational and overt aggression in preschool. *Developmental Psychology, 33*(4), 579-588.
34. Crick, N. R., & Grotpeter, J. K. (1995). Relational aggression, gender, and social-psychological adjustment. *Child Development, 66*(3), 710-722.
35. Dahmes, V. M. (1993). *A Descriptive Study of Multicultural Elementary Student Playground Behaviors and Their Relationship to Gender, Age, Race and Socioeconomic Status.* ERIC ED 369 521.
36. Galen, B. R., & Underwood, M. K. (1997). A developmental investigation of social aggression among children. *Developmental Psychology, 33*(4), 589-600.
37. Gropper, N., & Froschl, M. (1999). *The Role of Gender in Young Children's Teasing and Bullying Behavior.* ERIC ED 431 162.
38. Grossman, H., & Grossman, S. H. (1994). *Gender Issues in Education.* Needham, MA: Allyn & Bacon.
39. Henington, C., Hughes, J. N., Cavell, T. A., & Thompson, B. (1998). The role of relational aggression in identifying aggressive boys and girls. *Journal of School Psychology, 36*(4), 57-77.
40. Hyun, E., & Tyler, M. (1999). *Examination of Preschool Teachers' Biased Perception on Gender Differences.* ERIC ED 429 711.
41. Lansford, J. E., & Parker, J. G. (1999). Children's interaction in triads: Behavioral profiles and effects of gender patterns of friendship among members. *Developmental Psychology, 35*(1), 80-93.
42. Owens, L. D. (1995). *Aggression in Schools. Gender and Developmental Differences.* ERIC ED 404 592.
43. Paquette, J. A., & Underwood, M. K. (1999). Gender differences in young adolescents' experiences of peer victimization: Social and physical aggression. *Merrill-Palmer Quarterly, 45*(2), 242-266.
44. Rys, G. S., & Bear, G. G. (1997). Relational aggression and peer Relations: Gender and developmental issues. *Merrill-Palmer Quarterly, 43*(1), 87-106.

45. Tannen, D. (1990). *You Just Don't Understand.* New York: William Morrow.
46. Twarek, L. S., & George, H. S. (1994). *Gender Differences During Recess in Elementary School.* ERIC ED 381 277.
47. Wakefield, W. D., Smith, T., DeMorat, M., Britsch, B., Su-Je, C., & Hudley, C. (1997). *Perceptions of Aggressive Behavior: A Look Across Grade, Sex and School.* ERIC ED 408 075.
48. Zeman, J., & Shipman, K. (1996). Children's expression of negative affect: Reasons and methods. *Developmental Psychology, 32*(5), 842-849.

Chapter 5

NON-DISCRIMINATORY INSTRUCTION

When special education educators employ only the teaching styles they are most comfortable using they meet the needs of some students, usually middle-class European Americans, and discriminate against many others. They can avoid such discrimination by adapting their instructional methods to the cultural, contextual, and linguistic diversity among their students.

CULTURAL CHARACTERISTICS

Exceptional students' cultural backgrounds influence their learning styles (1-18). The ways students relate to adults and their peers at home and in their communities affects the way they function in school. Some children are brought up to be active participants in the learning process. Other children are expected to be less active and more passive recipients of instruction and information. African American students tend to learn more effectively in an interactive, participatory learning environment, whereas many Hispanic Americans, and Asian and Pacific Island American students are expected to be passive learners. The following quotations describe the passive learning styles of Hispanic Americans and Southeast Asian Americans.

The Hispanic culture requires good students to be passive learners—to sit quietly at their desks, pay attention, learn what they are taught and speak only when they are called upon. Anglo educational methods often require students

69

to be active students–to show initiative and leadership, to volunteer questions and answers, and to question the opinion of others. (9, p. 207)

> Since they have been taught to learn by listening, watching (observing), and imitating, these students may have a difficult time adjusting to learning by active doing and discovering. . . . There is a lesser emphasis, as compared to the American school system, on critical thinking and judgmental questions. If a teacher were to ask a question on the relationship between two concepts, one might see Indochinese students searching through their notes or books for the answers, or they may display reluctance or discomfort. (14, p. 42)

Although active participatory learning is a very effective instructional approach, students who are not comfortable with this method may require a great deal of direction and supervision during self-directed activities until they become comfortable with a more active role.

Cultures differ in terms of the degree of personal involvement teachers are supposed to have with their students. In some cultures, educators' interest in and involvement with students are expected to be restricted to their functioning in school. In other cultures, teachers are expected to be interested and involved with them as persons who are also students. The following quote explains why Native American students, among others, may learn more when their teachers show interest in their out of school life:

"Village students tend to expect highly personalized, emotionally intense relationships . . . with their teachers. . . . Village students consider it legitimate to expect a teacher to 'care about' them as total persons, not as learners of a particular subject matter" (12, p. 312).

As noted in the previous chapter, there are significant ethnic and gender differences in the extent to which students are trained to accomplish things on their own and to arrive at their own independent opinions and decisions, or are brought up to be dependent on the aid, support, opinions, and feedback of their parents and other adults. Compared to European American students, many students of color, especially Hispanic Americans, Native Americans, Filipino, and Southeast Asian Americans tend to be more interested in obtaining their teachers' direction and feedback.

As noted in the previous chapter, cultures differ in the degree to which they stress cooperation, competition, and individualism. Some students are taught to be competitive with their peers. Other students brought up to expect and count on the help and the cooperation of others and to reciprocate in kind. African Americans, Asian and Pacific Island Americans, Filipino Americans, Hawaiian Americans, Hispanic Americans, and European American females, especially those from poor backgrounds, tend to be brought up to be cooperative, whereas European American males tend to respond better to competitive and individualistic situations.

The positive results of cooperative learning on many students' achievement, attitudes, and interpersonal relationships has been demonstrated repeatedly (10). Typically, interethnic relationships improve, students learn more, get along better with their peers, and feel better about themselves when they learn in cooperative environments. However, this does not apply to all students. Some students are less receptive than others to these approaches and may have difficulty adjusting to working in groups or committees.

Although no culture expects children to be completely individualistic or group oriented, there are important cultural differences in the degree to which these relationship styles are emphasized. In some cultures, children are brought up to be relatively individualistic. Such children prefer to work alone and to rely only on themselves to accomplish their goals and deal with challenges, difficulties, and problems. When they are assigned to groups, in comparison to more group-oriented students, they are likely to continue to work independently neither soliciting nor offering assistance. Although they may not be competitive with their peers, students who prefer to work alone may require considerable assistance before they can function well in cooperative learning environments.

All children without visual or auditory impairments learn both visually and aurally. Nevertheless, there are significant culturally influenced differences among students. It is important for special education educators to know whether students' cultures prepare people to be primarily aural learners, like many Native Americans, or visual learners, like many African Americans, Hispanic Americans, Haitian Americans and Hmong Americans, because this would enable them to adapt their instructional techniques to students' needs.

Students' ability to sit still for long periods of time is greatly influenced by their cultural background. In general, African American students are more active and less able to adjust to the sedentary learning environments of American schools than are European Americans.

> In many American schools and especially in inner city schools, children are expected to talk or to move about only when directed to do so by teachers. . . . Those children who talk and move about with or without teacher directions do not meet normative standards and expectations. . . . Euro-American children possess the movement repertoire that will satisfy the normative standards and expectations governing child behavior in elementary classrooms while the richer movement repertoire of Black children does not satisfy those normative standards. (1, pp. 610)

Knowledge of whether youngsters are expected to sit in a quiet and controlled manner in most situations, or are allowed to be active and noisy enables special education educators to use instructional techniques that both permit students a level of activity that approximates what they are accustomed to and provide them with ways to discharge their energy. Such knowledge also helps special education educators to distinguish between students who are truly hyperactive and those whose highly active behavior patterns are culturally influenced.

Students also differ in terms of whether they function better in highly stimulating or more calm learning environments. African American and Hispanic American students are used to more stimulation than students typically experience in school. That may be why African American and Hispanic American students perform better and achieve more when the curriculum includes many different materials, makes frequent use of nonverbal instructional forms such as visual media or manipulative games, and allows students more autonomy than in classrooms that are teacher controlled, use a great deal of verbal learning, and involve limited use of different materials.

> Many African American children are exposed to high-energy, fast-paced home environments, where there is simultaneous variable stimulation (e.g., televisions and music playing simultaneously and people talking and moving in and about the home freely). Hence, low-energy, monolithic environments (as seen in many traditional school environments) are less stimulating. . . . Variety in instruction provides the spirit and enthusiasm for learning. When instructional strategies facilitate stimulus variety, using combinations of oral, print, and visual media, African-American students perform better. Instructional activities should include music, singing, and movement. (8, pp. 118-119)

In some cultures children tend to learn by trial and error. They observe, read about, or are told how something is done. Then they practice it under the supervision of a more knowledgeable and skilled individual. Learners are expected to make mistakes because "practice makes perfect." In other cultures individuals are expected to continue to watch how something is done as many times and for as long as necessary until they feel they can do it. Only when they are sure they can succeed do they demonstrate their ability to others.

Students who grow up in trial-and-error cultures can usually take in stride the mistakes they make in public when they volunteer answers or are called on. Those who are accustomed to a "watch then do" approach have greater difficulty expressing themselves in public while they are learning from their mistakes.

Students who are uncomfortable with trial-and-error learning and exposing their errors to others may need special educators to not pressure them to try things before they are ready to do so. This may be a difficult adjustment for special education educators who believe that most students with learning and cognitive disabilities, sensory impairments, or emotional problems need someone to encourage them to try to do things when they are unsure of themselves.

Although all cultures use many different teaching techniques with children, only in some cultures do adults teach children by raising leading questions about their beliefs to guide them to a more correct or accurate understanding of things. In other cultures, children are accustomed to being told what is correct and unaccustomed to having their beliefs questioned critically.

> In the Anglo-dominated school system, the child is encouraged, even pressured, both to ask and analyze questions. . . . There is consequently a built-in clash between the ethnic (Raza) home tradition and the Anglo school tradition of constant and formal questioning. The WASP "inquisition" would be highly hostile to the Mexican-American attitude of tolerance. (4, p. 64)

As a result, special education educators may have to consider students' learning styles when deciding whether, how often, and with which students to use instructional approaches that involve debates, analysis of controversial topics, and the examination of students' opinions and beliefs.

All students would rather succeed than fail and learn to read than remain illiterate. However, because their cultural backgrounds help shape their perceptions about the value and role of education, they also have different motives for succeeding. Some students desire to succeed academically, to go to college, to earn a lot of money, and be successful materialistically. Some strive to succeed to receive honor and prestige. Others may believe it is important to learn for its own sake. As noted previously, some African American and Hispanic American students, especially poor, males lose their motivation to try to succeed because they are alienated, distrustful, angry, and disillusioned about the schools they attend and the teachers that instruct them. Some students are pressured by their peers not to conform or to do well in school because to do so is to "act White." In addition, they purposefully avoid academic success by cutting school and not studying.

Although the evidence is somewhat inconsistent, it appears that some European American, Hispanic American, and Asian and Pacific Island American females, especially those from less affluent and poor backgrounds, have mixed feelings about and are uncomfortable with success in courses or occupations traditionally thought of as being in the male domain (10). They may be concerned that they will seem less feminine and be less popular with males if they outperform them in these areas or believe that a female's place is in the home.

Because of these differences, special education educators should not assume that all their students are equally motivated to succeed in school. They should learn about each student's motivation and then decide how to handle each individual case. This may be a difficult task for regular education teachers who have many students in their classes; the lower student-teacher ratios that prevail in special education make this goal quite feasible.

All children in all cultures must learn many abstract concepts. However, some cultures deemphasize abstract learning and are more people oriented. As a result, some students are more interested in solving math problems about people than those that involve only numerical computations and human geography (how people live) rather than physical geography (rivers, topography, etc.). African Americans and Native Americans tend to be people oriented. "In comparison to the Anglo culture, the Hispanic culture emphasizes people over ideas. . . . As a result some Hispanic students may relate better to a person-centered rather than thing- (or idea-centered curriculum" (9, p. 65).

Research has suggested that white children are very object-oriented. That is, they have numerous opportunities to manipulate objects and discover properties and relationships. Consequently, this society's educational system is very object oriented. Classrooms are filled with educational hardware and technology. . . . Research with black children, in contrast, has found them to be very people-oriented. Most black children grow up in large families where they have a great deal of human interaction. . . . When this cultural trait is acknowledged, the result will be more human interaction in the learning process. (11, pp. 19-20)

Because time is a primary concern in the United States, it is easy to assume that all cultures have similar attitudes about time. This, however, is not the case. There are significant differences in the extent to which people sacrifice present satisfactions for future goals. Although all ethnic groups are concerned about and prepare for the future, some are more present than future oriented.

The time many Mexican Americans value most is the present. Finishing a conversation with an old friend may be more important than keeping an appointment with a doctor. Making plans for the future may be less important than living to the fullest at the moment in hand. Many Mexican Americans perceive the time-serving ways of the Anglo as a misappropriation of the present. . . . The entire system of American education revolves about a ritualistic adherence to the ticking of the clock. What is the Mexican American child's reaction to the rigid schedules and the incessant pressures to plan for the future? How does he view a reward system that is programmed to respond to him at six week intervals? (7, p. 641)

Pacific peoples have learned to focus on meeting present needs and expecting little change. Americans value change, are future oriented, and expect that objectives will be achieved as a result of hard work. (3, p. 264)

Other groups including European Americans and some Asian and Pacific Island Americans tend to be more future oriented. Because individuals differ in these respects, it is important to know whether students can work toward the accomplishment of long-term goals and rewards, or are more responsive to short-term goals, immediate satisfaction, and immediate reinforcement.

Most European American students are accustomed to starting tasks when they are supposed to, and completing them within a specified time period. African Americans, Hispanic American, and Native Americans, among others tend to have a much more flexible attitude about time and punctuality, and therefore some of them have a difficult time learning in schools with inflexible time schedules and routines.

As noted in the previous chapter, many students of color are accustomed to working at a slower pace than their European American teachers expect. Expecting them to work at the same pace and accomplish the same amount of work in a given time period as other students is counterproductive. On the other hand, allowing slow-working students to start early or providing them with additional time to finish their work in school or at home helps solve their problems. Moreover, not devaluing their work because it has taken them more time to complete it than other students or is handed in after a teacher-imposed deadline is the fair way to judge the results of their efforts. Likewise, rewarding students for the amount of work they accomplish—how many problems or pages they complete within a given time period, rather than the quality of their work may unwittingly cause slow-working students to make mistakes and give students the message that it is more important to complete something fast than to do it correctly.

Although children and youth share many interests in common, students from different backgrounds have somewhat different interests. What is said next about African American students applies equally well to many other groups of students.

> Most African-American children sit in classrooms, yet are outside the information being discussed. The white child sits in the middle of the information, whether it is literature, history, politics or art. The task of the Afrocentric curriculum is finding patterns in African-American history and culture that help the teacher place the child in the middle of the intellectual experience. This is not an idea to replace all things European, but to expand the dialogue to include African-American information. (2, p. 46)

To avoid this type of discrimination, special education educators should organize their curricula around the interests of all students. They should include all their cultures regularly, not in special units or on special occasions like Black History Month, Martin Luther King's birthday, or Cinco de Mayo. As the following author points out, "Setting aside a month for black history or women's history seems strange and artificial to most students regardless of color. These children aren't naive. What are the other seven months: White Male History Month?" (6, p. 14).

CONTEXTUAL CHARACTERISTICS

Special education educators who disregard the contextual problems of their immigrant, migrant, rural, and homeless students when they instruct them discriminate against them. However, adapting instructional approaches to their contextual characteristics helps these students to succeed in spite of their problems.

Immigrant and refugee exceptional students require a great deal of help to succeed in school (19, 20). Including aspects of the students' cultures in the classroom by putting up pictures of their native countries; arranging for classroom demonstrations of the cooking, music, or dancing of the students' places of birth; and discussing the students' countries of origin can overcome their culture shock, make the classroom environment a little less strange, and help smooth their transitions.

Providing alternatives when students are not ready for coed recreational activities, competitive games, showering nude in front of others, and so on can sometimes prevent students from having unpleasant experiences. Offering alternative foods and snacks to replace food that students' religions prohibit them from eating or they are unaccustomed to eating can show concern and respect for them and their customs.

Culture brokers—bicultural individuals, usually other students, assistant teachers, paraprofessionals, or parent volunteers who are equally knowledgeable about and comfortable in both the students' culture and the culture of the school—can assist immigrant students to adjust to unfamiliar school environments. Culture brokers help bridge the gap between the schools and students' of color cultures by performing three roles. As translators to students, they teach students which behaviors are appropriate in various situations, explain the possible motivations behind European Americans' actions or their reactions to the students' behavior, and so on. As translators to the school, they help the students' teachers and peers understand and appreciate the students feelings, attitudes, motives, and behavior. As models, they demonstrate the appropriate behavior necessary to be successful in the new culture. The following statement by a Peruvian American student illustrates the usefulness of a cultural broker.

My first day in school I didn't understand anything at all. I didn't speak English, I didn't understand the Black students. I didn't understand the white students and there were hardly any Latinos. I was real scared. Then they assigned me a buddy. She was Black and Latino like me and she was in the eighth grade too. I went to all of her classes with her and never went anywhere during recess, lunch, or any time without her.

She told me that the other students were trying to figure out what I was, Black, Latino or what. I looked like I could be Black but didn't speak or act Black. She helped me understand things. She taught me what to do when people started up with me. She taught me how to do things right in school. And she explained why the Black kids acted that way.

Little by little I learned how to act in school. I even learned how to be Black. Now I can act Latino, Black or white. (19)

Cultural assimilators can help students who are unfamiliar with American school practices understand and adjust to them (20). Cultural assimilators typically consist of a series of problematic situations with a number of alternate ways of behaving in the situation or perceiving the situation. Students discuss each alternative's advantages and disadvantages, appropriateness or inappropriateness, accuracy or inaccuracy in the United States. For example, students are asked to discuss what they should do if they are sitting in the classroom talking with classmates when the teacher enters the room, what they should do if they do not understand something while the teacher is talking to the class, or what they would do when they will not able to complete a homework assignment the teacher gives for the next day.

Immigrant exceptional students' academic readiness skills and knowledge are usually different from those of most students in their classes. If they have not attended school prior to coming to the United States they will lack a great deal of knowledge and skill that children acquire in school. If they attended school irregularly there will be huge gaps in what they know and can do. Even if they attended regularly they will not have learned many of the things that are included in the curriculum of the typical U.S. school.

Therefore it is essential to provide these students with a curriculum that is as individualized to their needs as possible. This can be done by starting at the student's current level of functioning, including the concepts and skills the student has acquired, being on the lookout for and filling in gaps, and using teaching techniques that complement the student's learning styles.

Like immigrant students, migrant exceptional students require a great deal of support. The following suggestions for adapting instructional approaches to the context of migrants students' lives appear repeatedly in the literature (5, 21-24).

- Utilize a multicultural approach to make the classroom more relevant to students and to help students bridge the gap between their experiences and the culture of the school.
- Include English as a second language instruction, sheltered English approaches, and bilingual paraprofessionals to facilitate limited English proficient students' academic learning and their acquisition of English language skills.
- Do not assume that migrant students have been receiving the special education assistance they need on a regular basis because they move from school to school. Identify the academic problems students experience because of their disabilities and their irregular school attendance and furnish them with the individual assistance they need.
- Provide students with successful role models by inviting individuals who have escaped from the vicious cycle many migrant families are caught in to be guest speakers, tutors, and so on.
- Help students become acquainted with the community, the services the community offers, and how their life can be improved by making use of those services.
- Provide students with opportunities to learn career and vocational skills other than farm work that will increase their employability.
- Encourage and assist parents to become involved in their children's education. Even if parents are unable to help students with their school work because they themselves have not attended or succeeded in school, their children learn more when their parents are interested in and discuss their children's education with them.

Homeless students with disabilities need a great deal of understanding and support from their teachers to cope with the realities of their lives. The following suggestions have been offered by experts in the field (25-31).

- Focus on making sure students' basic needs are met. Students who are struggling with problems of transportation to school, food, clothing, sleep, and school supplies are unable to give their all to their studies. Assist students and their families to obtain the social, medical, financial, and other support services they require. Be discreet to avoid embarrassing them. Use techniques that empower parents to deal with these agencies to strengthen their childcare role and foster more positive parent-child relationships. However, if necessary, advocate for families who meet with resistance from service agencies.

• Provide students a safe environment in which they can feel secure, relax their guard, act their age, and be themselves. Runaway and homeless students often have learned to distrust adults who may have been unable or unwilling to care for them. They may be on their guard against anticipated disappointments, rejections and abuse. They may have had to assume adultlike responsibilities before they were ready to do so.

• Assign students personal space. Because homeless and runaway students are unlikely to have space of their own—their own room, closet, bed, place at a dinner table, and so on—providing them with a space in their classroom that they can call their own and mark with symbols of their identity can improve their sense of self-worth and stability.

• Assess students' skills, knowledge, abilities, strengths, and weaknesses in great detail. Although this is desirable for all students with disabilities, it is especially important for students who attend school irregularly, enroll in many different schools, and often do not complete assignments when they do attend.

• Encourage and assist students to become autonomous and independent so that they come to believe that they can be in control of their own lives.

• Maintain the kinds of flexibility necessary to incorporate students into your program for whatever amount of time they are able to attend. Allowing students to progress at their own pace, individualizing their assignments, using modules and computerized instruction are tools that can provide needed flexibility.

• Encourage and assist students to attend your program even when it becomes difficult for them to do so. However, do not penalize students who are unable to attend, complete assignments, and so on because of contextual problems.

• Work closely with other agencies that are assisting your students and their families. Collaborative efforts are more effective than individualistic uncoordinated approaches.

LINGUISTIC CHARACTERISTICS

Limited English proficient exceptional students and students who speak nonstandard English dialects should be instructed in a linguistically appropriate manner. Those who are not proficient in English require bilingual special education services—instruction for part of the day in their native languages while they are learning English. Bilingual education helps limited English proficient students learn more efficiently and function better in schools where almost every transaction is in English and reduces the likelihood that they will become frustrated, angry, anxious, or resentful. If bilingual special education is unavailable, English-as-a-second-language and sheltered English approaches can be used effectively. Limited English proficient exceptional students should never be placed in a classroom taught only in English that is not adapted to their needs.

Special education educators need to avoid prejudice against nonstandard English dialects. They should not correct or demean the way the students speak. Nonstandard English speaking students can express themselves as well as standard English speakers and learn to read and write standard English without learning to speak standard English.

REFERENCES

These references discuss how students' cultural characteristics affect their learning styles:

1. Almanza, H. P., & Mosley, W. J. (1980). Cultural adaptations and modifications for culturally diverse handicapped children. *Exceptional Children, 46*(8), 608-614.
2. Asante, M. K. (1991). Putting Africa at the center. *Newsweek, 118*(13), 46.
3. Brady, M. P., & Anderson, D. D. (1983). Some issues in the implementation of P.L. 94-142 in the Pacific Basin Territories. *Education, 103*(3), 259-269.

4. Burger, H. G. (1972). Ethno-lematics: Evoking "shy' Spanish-American pupils by cross-cultural mediation. *Adolescence, 6*(25), 61-76.
5. Condon, E. C., Peters, J. Y., & Sueiro-Ross, C. (1979). *Special Education and the Hispanic Child: Cultural Perspectives.* Philadelphia: Temple University, Teacher Corps Mid-Atlantic Network.
6. Elrich, M. (1994). The stereotype within. *Educational Leadership, 51*(8), 12-15.
7. Felder, D. (1970). The education of Mexican Americans: Fallacies of the Monocultural approach. *Social Education, 34*(6), 639-642.
8. Franklin, M. E. (1992). Culturally sensitive instructional practices for African-American learners with disabilities. *Exceptional Children, 59*(2), 115-122.
9. Grossman, H. (1995a). *Educating Hispanic Students: Implications for Instruction, Classroom Management, Counseling,and Assessment* (2nd ed.) Springfield, IL: Charles C Thomas, Publisher, Ltd..
10. Grossman, H. (1995b). *Special Education in a Diverse Society.* Boston: Allyn & Bacon.
11. Hale, J. (1978). Cultural influences on learning styles of Afro-American children. In L. Morris, G. Sather, & S. Scull (Eds.), *Extracting Learning Styles from Social/Cultural Diversity: A Study of Five American Minorities.* Norman, OK: Southwest Teacher Corps Network.
12. Hilliard, A. (1976). *Alternatives to I. Q. Testing: An Approach to the Identification of Gifted Minority Children.* Sacramento, CA: California State Department of Education.
13. Jaramillo, M. L. (1973). *Cautions When Working with the Culturally Different Child.* ERIC ED 115 622.
14. Kang-Ning, C. (1981). Education for Chinese and Indochinese. *Theory into Practice, 20*(1), 35-44.
15. Kantrowitz, B. (1991). A is for ashanti, b is for black. *Newsweek, 118*(13), 45-48.
16. Lewis, J., Vang, L., & Cheng, L. L. (1989). Identifying the language-learning difficulties of Hmong students: Implications of context and culture. *Topics in Language Disorders, 9*(3), 21-37.
17. More, A. J. (1987). Native Indian learning styles: A review for researchers and teachers. *Journal of American Indian Education, 27*(1), 17-29.
18. Rhodes, R. W. (1988). Holistic/teaching learning for Native American students. *Journal of American Indian Education, 27*(2), 21-29.

The contextual problems of immigrant students is the focus of these references:

19. Aranguri-Oshiro, R. (1987). Personal communication.
20. Ford, C. K., & Silverman, A. M. (1981). *American Cultural Encounters.* San Francisco: Alemany Press.

Migrant workers educational problems and their solutions are described in the following references:

21. Dyson, D. D. (1983). *Migrant Education: Utilizing Available Resources at the Local Level.* Las Cruces, NM: ERIC/CRESS.

22. Lawless, Ken. (1986). *Neediest of the Needy: Special Education for Migrants. Harvesting the Harvesters. Book 8.* ERIC ED 279 473.

23. Mattera, G. (1987). *Models of Effective Migrant Education Programs.* Las Cruces, NM: New Mexico State University, ERIC/CRESS.

24. Reynolds, C. J., & Salend, S. J. (1990). Issues and programs in the delivery of special education services to migrant students with disabilities. *Journal of Educational Issues of Language Minority Students, 7,* 69-83.

Solutions to homeless students' educational problems are described in these references:

25. Bassuk, E. L., & Gallagher, E. M. (1990). The impact of homelessness on children. In N. A. Boxill (Ed.), *Homeless Children: The Watchers and the Waiters.* Binghamton, NY: Haworth.

26. Burns, S. (Ed.). (1991). Homelessness demographics, causes and trends. *Homewords, 3*(4), 1-3.

27. Cavazos, L. F. (1990). *U. S. Department of Education Report to Congress on the Education for Homeless Children and Youth Program for the Period October 1, 1988 through September 30, 1989.* Washington, DC: U. S. Department of Education.

28. Heflin, L. J., & Rudy, K. (1991). *Homeless and in Need of Special Education.* Reston, VA: Council for Exceptional Children.

29. Rafferty, Y., & Rollins, N. (1990). *Homeless Children: Educational Challenges for the 1990's.* ERIC ED 325 589.

30. Russell, S. C., & Williams, E. U. (1988). Homeless handicapped children: A special education perspective. *Children's Environments Quarterly, 5*(1), 3-7.

31. Stronge, J. H., & Tenhouse, C. (1990). *Educating Homeless Children: Issues and Answers.* Bloomington, IN: Phi Delta Kappa Educational Foundation.

Chapter 6

NON-DISCRIMINATORY CLASSROOM MANAGEMENT

ACCEPTING CONTEXTUALLY INFLUENCED BEHAVIOR

Through no fault of their own, many exceptional students confront contextual problems that cause them to behave in ways that special educators find objectionable (1-5). Because students have no ability to control the conditions in which they live, special education educators may have to accept a certain amount of problematic behavior while they and others assist them to learn other ways of reacting to their difficulties.

Exceptional students who immigrate to the United States often behave in unexpected ways because of the culture shock they suffer when they have to adjust to a culture that is significantly different from their own. Not knowing what is expected of them, unable to solve interpersonal problems and unaware of what is and is not acceptable behavior in their new culture, they can become confused, anxious, and frustrated. Sad or depressed over the loss of their familiar way of life, they can withdraw from their teachers and the other students. Or they may become frustrated with and angry at people whose behavior they cannot understand and react aggressively toward them.

The plight of a Hispanic American student who suffers culture shock is described next.

> The very first day in the first grade the Mexican American child starts with a handicap no humane society should place on the shoulders of a mere child. English is the language of the classroom. He speaks no English or he speaks inadequate English. The whole program is designed to make him an Anglo. . .

. He doesn't want to become an Anglo or he doesn't know how. . . . The Anglo concepts and values that prevail are unintelligible to him. . . . There is nothing in the atmosphere from which he can draw any comfort. Nothing he can relate to. . . . He is one scared kid. (5, p. 3)

The suggestions in Chapter 5 can assist special education educators to lessen the impact of cultural shock on exceptional students. However, students may still react in problematic ways for a time. If they do, special education educators should accept as much of their behavior as possible without infringing on the rights of other students.

Refugee, homeless, and abused exceptional students among others may come to school with a great deal of fear and anxiety. Students who do not feel secure in their new surroundings, who are frightened by physical aggression or threats of aggression or even verbal conflicts among students may need to feel that their teachers will protect them from the possibility that they will get caught up in these events. Special education educators should do their best to make school a safe haven for them. If they are unable to handle discussions of themes such as war, starvation, crime, and so on, they may need to be allowed to engage in another activity or leave the class until the discussions have terminated.

Many immigrant exceptional students may experience identity conflicts during the acculturation process if they are pressured at home and in their community to maintain the traditional values of their culture while at the same time they are expected to accept the cultural values of the school. They may act out against their teachers and others who are the sources of their conflicts. A Chinese American high school student who immigrated to the United States when she was ten years old expressed her identity conflict in this way.

I don't know who I am. Am I the good Chinese daughter? Am I an American teenager? I always feel I am letting my parents down when I am with my friends because I act so American, but I also feel that I will never really be an American. I never feel really comfortable with myself anymore. (3, p. 30)

Immigrant exceptional students are usually poorly prepared to succeed in their new schools. Many of them have not attended school before they arrived in the United States. Those that have, often have not studied the things that most special education educators and school administrators expect and value. As a result, they may be very far behind. Frustrated by trying to produce at the level of the other students, they may act out their anger by behaving in ways that are disruptive to other students. Or they may give up trying, withdraw, and tune out their teachers.

Native American exceptional students who grow up on reservations and attend schools run by and designed for European American students are in a position that is somewhat analogous to that of immigrant students. They too live in a region separate from mainstream America where they speak a language other than English. They too are ill prepared to adjust to and profit from the education typically offered in mainstream schools. This is especially true if the curriculum is culturally irrelevant, encourages beliefs and values that conflict with those of their communities, and is taught by teachers who are unfamiliar with their culture and unable to speak their native languages.

Rural children who migrate to urban areas often have similar experiences and require similar approaches. The following problems have tended to characterize many Appalachian students and their families who have moved to urban northern cities.

> Appalachian youth are less likely to seek, or readily accept, school personnel support such as sponsorship or encouragement by a particular teacher or counselor. . . . They are less likely to participate in school activities.
>
> Youth do not identify with their schools especially in junior and senior high school, since most youth are placed in an unfamiliar neighborhood. . . . Familism requires that family situations take priority over education. . . . High absenteeism is at least in part a result of youth being needed at home to help care for siblings and household matters. The traditional migration process, in the three to five years after initial settlement in urban areas . . . can mean moving several times to find satisfactory neighborhoods, jobs, schools, doctors, and shopping areas. . . Parents may encourage students into career/practical skills and vocational classes rather than college preparatory or advanced placement classes. . . . Class differences cause Appalachian youth to feel "looked down on" and the lack of attention given to Appalachian culture only adds to a defeated self-image. Differences in language, dress, and values are seen by other classes as deficiencies or inferiority. (2, pp. 99-101)

Many immigrants and most refugees arrive in the United States with few economic resources to support them. As a result many of them move into relatively impoverished environments that can seriously impede their ability to succeed in school.

Immigrants tend to settle in relatively deteriorating areas of inner cities where educational facilities are already poor and heavily used. In the absence of sufficient additional assistance, the influx of immigration adds an almost unbearable burden on the resources of the school. The home living condition of immigrant children is equally a serious drawback in terms of learning environment. Many of these immigrants live in crowded houses and apartments occupied by more than one family. The children may have no quiet place at home to do their homework or to study. (4, p. 7)

Students with these kinds of contextual problems cannot behave like their peers. Pressuring them to behave "correctly" only makes matters worse. On the other hand, accepting their behavior as much as possible provides them with the breathing space they need to adjust to their new schools at their own paces.

Some exceptional students misbehave in class because of the relationship between the students' ethnic or socioeconomic group and the group the teacher represents to them, usually the European Americans. Students who have personally experienced prejudice, oppression, rejection, or abuse by European Americans or who have been brought up to anticipate and be wary of such treatment may be suspicious of the teacher's motives. This certainly could apply to African American, Hispanic, and Native American students who have experienced the discriminatory treatment described in Chapter 1.

Students who are alienated, hostile, and suspicious of another group such as the dominant society and its institutions and organizations can bring this hostility to school. They may disbelieve and reject out of hand much of what they are taught in class. Even at a young age, they may already disbelieve the concept "your friend, the police officer." As they progress through the grades, they may reject both their teachers' and the textbooks' interpretations of American and world history—the role of Christopher Columbus, the causes of the Civil War, the desirability of American intervention in other countries, as well as the standard explanations of how the U.S. economic and political systems function. Their opinions about the best way to solve the current issues facing the United States and the world may be at odds with those of their teachers. They may believe, sometimes with justification, that their teachers are insensitive to their cultural needs and indifferent, or even prejudiced toward them. As a result, they may be suspicious of their teachers' motives.

Although some students keep their feelings to themselves in class, many others–especially the older ones–act them out.

In doing so, they may repeatedly challenge their teachers' statements and demonstrate a lack of respect and disregard for their authority by not following rules, acting bored, making sarcastic and provocative comments, and purposely disrupting the class. Some students may withdraw from what they consider to be an irrelevant and prejudicial education by tuning their teachers out, arriving late, and cutting class.

Special education educators who are the recipient of their students' anger, resentment, and distrust of the system should tell students that they understand how they feel and why they might feel that way but explain how things are different in their classrooms. If students act out their anger or resentment in class, special education educators might tolerate behaviors that do not seriously disrupt the class while making it clear that although they understand how the students feel, they will not be allowed to interfere with other students' right to learn. When students withdraw from classroom participation, come late, cut classes, and so on, special education educators can explain that there are better ways of expressing their feelings and solving the problem than denying themselves an education. Earning these students' trust and confidence by utilizing a multicultural approach and advocating for their rights when they are mistreated or victimized by prejudice can also help gain their trust.

ACCEPTING CULTURALLY INFLUENCED BEHAVIOR

Students who do not share their teachers' cultural backgrounds can behave in ways that teachers may find unacceptable and even offensive (6-9). In some cultures, when people communicate they are expected to be considerate of other people's sensibilities. In other cultures, the right of individuals to express their feelings openly and frankly, regardless of how it might affect others, is considered more paramount, and people are expected to tolerate, accept, and deal with the expression of intense feelings. African Americans and European Americans tend to be very different in this regard.

Whites want social interaction to operate at an emotionally subdued level. To realize this goal they first establish the rule that expressive behavior shall be subdued, which develops sensibilities capable of tolerating only relatively subdued outputs. . . . Black cultural norms desire levels of public interaction that are more emotionally intense. Consequently they allow individuals to express themselves at the level at which feelings are felt. (8, p. 117)

Cultures have very different ideas about exactly what is honest communication and even whether honest communication is desirable. No culture expects people to be completely honest. Other issues besides honesty such as the relative importance placed by the culture on maintaining one's honor or one's face, avoiding disagreement and conflict, avoiding personal responsibility, and so on influence a group's opinion about how honest communication should be. In some cultures when people communicate it is more important to maintain smooth interpersonal relationships than to tell the truth.

Falsehood carries no moral structure for a Cambodian, Laotian, or Vietnamese. The essential question is not whether a statement is true or false, but what the intention of the statement is. Does it facilitate interpersonal harmony? Does it indicate a wish to change the subject? Hence, one must learn the "heart' of the speaker through his/her words. (9, pp. 6, 7)

In some cultures, a promise to do something or to comply with an expectation may not be meant literally. If a refusal would lead to an awkward or uncomfortable interpersonal moment or insult a person, especially someone in a position of authority, a promise may be little more than a way of maintaining smooth interpersonal relationships. In some cultures people do not say when they are unwilling or unable to do something or when they disagree. Instead they maintain that they too feel or believe as others do and that they will do something to avoid an unpleasant moment. As a result, some students believe that making a promise they do not plan to fulfill and saying something that is not so are acceptable behaviors when doing so contributes to interpersonal harmony or helps someone save face. Students from these cultural backgrounds may not have the slightest intention of complying with a behavioral plan they have agreed to or a contingency contract they have signed and not think they have done anything reprehensible.

In our diverse society students from different cultural backgrounds have dissimilar ideas about acceptable group behavior. The following quote describes how group processes practiced by Hispanic Americans and African Americans can diverge from the typical European American approach.

> When a group of Hispanics disagree they may resolve the issue by continuing to discuss it until it becomes apparent that a consensus has been reached without polling the group or calling for a vote. . . .
>
> This is much better than bringing out the differences of opinion among people by requiring them to take a stand–stand up and be counted, show which side you're on etc. This can increase conflict and often does. (6, p. 124)
>
> In a heated discussion, blacks frequently make their points whenever they can enter the discussion. Deference is given to the person who considers his or her point most urgent. Turn-taking is the style of whites, who usually raise their hands to be recognized. Teachers find black students impolite, aggressive, and boisterous when they cut off another student or fail to restrain themselves so that every student can have a turn to talk. (7, p. 29)

In different cultures males and females express interest in one another in unique ways. What one group may consider an insulting form of attention or show of interest, other groups may deem acceptable. "Piropos," compliments said to females whom one does not know about how sexy they are or how great they look are acceptable in many Hispanic American communities, but insulting to many European Americans. This can create problems if European American teachers think that the piropos they may overhear are insults and react accordingly.

It is important for special education educators to recognize when their students' "undesirable" behavior is culturally influenced and not the result of willful misbehavior. They should accept culturally influenced behaviors that do not conflict with the effective operation of the educational process and change only those that do. When they choose to change culturally influenced behaviors they should not tell students that behaviors that are acceptable in their homes and communities are wrong or bad. Instead of requiring students' to reject the values, beliefs, and practices of their families and friends, they can help them to identify with and accept both cultural systems and prepare them to function one way at home and another way at school.

INTERPRETING STUDENTS' BEHAVIOR ACCURATELY

Special education educators can misperceive and misunderstand students' behaviors when they interpret them from their own perspectives (10-18). Many African Americans express their emotions much more intensely than most European Americans. When European American special education educators observe African Americans behaving aggressively and assertively, too many of the educators assume that the students are much angrier or upset than they actually are. Attributing a level of anger to African American students that would be correct for European American students who behaved in a similar way, the teachers can become uncomfortable, even anxious, and concerned about what they incorrectly anticipate will happen next. As a result, they intervene when no intervention is necessary. If educators appreciated the cultural context of African Americans' seemingly aggressive behavior toward others and understood that such behavior is unlikely to cause the physical fight or whatever else they expect to occur, they would be less likely to have to intervene to make themselves feel more at ease in the situation. This would lessen the likelihood that African Americans would get into trouble needlessly. As an African American professional sees it:

Most teachers are unprepared to accept the active, aggressive behavior of Black boys. The aggressive behavior of a Black child is immediately interpreted as hostile. The teacher's expectation is that the student should be compliant, docile, and responsive to authority. The student is expected to conform to a standard of behavior that the teacher is familiar with, the compliant child standard that was indicative of the teacher's up-bringing. It is as though the teacher makes an unwritten contract with the student, "If you don't behave, I won't (or can't) teach you."

The next step in the process is that the teacher will make futile attempts to control the aggressive, active behavior, but abandon those efforts very quickly and conclude that the child is unmanageable. The child resists the teacher's efforts to control the behavior. More often than not, the behavior becomes more unmanageable. As the disruptive behavior increases, the amount of time and effort available to devote to attending to the instructions and acquiring academic skills decreases. In all likelihood the student prefers to avoid the academic work. Within a short period of time it becomes apparent that this unmanageable student is not functioning at grade level. This then can be interpreted, depending on the tolerance level of the teachers, as a learning problem and a justification for referral for special placement. The longer the time span involved, the greater the learning problem. (10, pp. 78-79)

European American middle-class special education educators tend to be brought up to consider the effect of their actions on other people's sensibilities before acting. They typically teach their children and assume that all children are taught to be considerate of others, for example, by keeping the volume on the TV or stereo low so as to avoid disturbing others. The African American culture tends to stress people's individuality–their right to determine for themselves the way they satisfy their desires–and typically requires individuals to learn to tolerate the inconvenience the rights of others may create for them. Thus, African American children may have to be taught to be considerate of others by learning how to do what they have to do even when the volume on the TV or stereo is high. Teachers who are unaware of this difference may mistakenly believe that some African American students who are behaving appropriately for their culture are inconsiderate and self-centered, rather than merely behaving in a culturally approved manner.

> Whites have been taught that to act on behalf of their own feelings is unjustified if someone else's sensibilities might become offended as a result. So strongly ingrained is this rule that it has the force of a moral injunction. Rather than violate it and feel guilty . . . whites will hold back what they truly feel even if this will result in an injustice to their feelings or create for themselves an unwanted social situation.
>
> From a Black standpoint, individuals asserting themselves in accordance with their feelings are seen not as violating the sacred rights of others but, rather, as preserving the sacred rights of self. (8, pp. 121, 123)

European Americans and African Americans tend to have somewhat different ideas about how students and others should behave in groups. An African American educator describes how group behavior patterns that are acceptable in the African community can cause problems for students in school.

> Blacks are accustomed to integrating mental, emotional, and physical activities. Schools tend to encourage compartmentalizing these areas. The Black child's involvement in cognitive classroom activities is likely to be signaled by vocal responses, exuberance, and physical movement. Teachers consider this behavior disruptive because they expect that one can be highly stimulated to intellectual activities without involving affective or psychomotor dimensions.
>
> What teachers view as total chaos and noise may be structured activity to Blacks. What teachers consider planned activities may be perceived by Black

students as prohibiting constraints. The problem of perception stems from different sets of expectations and cultural sensibilities. (11, pp. 32-33)

Elaborating on the way Blacks respond to others when they are reciting, performing, and so on, Gay and Abrahams state:

> There is more total interaction involved; all those in the social environment must play some active response role if it is only through such responses as "right on brother."
>
> The Black child in performing looks for verbal and kinesthetic support from his peers. The teacher hears noise and is threatened. The child's success is measured by his peers by the extent to which he stimulates the others to provide responses. When this behavior is manifested, teachers see an undisciplined and discourteous group of Blacks.
>
> This situation arises because contrarily in white, middle-class culture the relationship between a performer and his audience demands a show of passivity on the part of the latter. . . . When Black children's classroom behavior is assessed using this frame of reference, the conclusions are foreordained. The culturally-influenced Black ways of demonstrating interest and involvement are interpreted as restlessness, inattentiveness, and sometimes hostility. (12, p. 338)

The following quotations provide insight into the kinds of cultural misperceptions educators can make with exceptional Asian and Pacific Island American students.

> The child does not volunteer to answer. He just sits and waits for his teacher to call upon him. So in the eyes of the American teacher, Asian children, as compared to the American students, are dull, passive, unresponsive, and lack initiative. Most of the time, Chinese (Asian) students are ignored because of their absolute silence in class. (17, p. 11)

American straightforwardness is considered at best impolite, if not brutal. In Indochina, one does not come directly to the point. To do so is, for an American, a mark of honesty and forthrightness while a person from Indochina sees it as a lack of intelligence or courtesy. Falsehood carries no moral structure for a Cambodian, Laotian, or Vietnamese. The essential question is not whether a statement is true or false, but what the intention of the statement is. Does it facilitate interpersonal harmony? Does it indicate a wish to change the subject? Hence, one must learn the "heart" of the speaker through his/her words. In Indochina, one thinks very carefully before speaking. The American style of "speaking one's mind" is thus misunderstood.

> The Vietnamese literal equivalent of the English word "Yes" is "Da" (pronounced "Ya" in the Southern Vietnamese dialect). However, whereas the English "Yes" means unequivocally "Yes," the Vietnamese "Da" means a variety of things. In the final analysis, it can mean "Yes," but in general usage it merely means "I am politely listening to you," and it does not at all mean that "I agree with you." The listener may disagree with what he hears, but due to his politeness, cannot say no. His English "Yes" for him conveys the polite and noncommittal Vietnamese "Da," but to the American it can carry only its English meaning. Thus, the Vietnamese may appear insincere, or even stupid, to the American. (9, pp. 6, 7, 19)

It is easy to understand how educators who do not know these facts could think their students really agreed to do what they have been asked to do and become angry and frustrated when the students don't follow through after saying "yes."

Commenting on the way European American teachers may misunderstand the behavior of Hispanic students, Jaramillo states that:

> An Anglo teacher is likely to consider many of the Spanish speaking children in his class dependent in a negative sense, or perhaps he will say they are immature, or that they are retarded in their social development. In reality, these differences are purely cultural, and viewed from another perspective, these children are perfectly normal and mature for their age. (13, p. 13)

Special education educators may mistakenly attribute behavior problems that are culturally-influenced to other causes. Some of the ways European American teachers can misunderstand the causes of African American students' behavior are revealed in the following description of the faculty of a desegregated school.

> The first and most basic teacher response to the number of problems presented by the Black children was to devise some personal explanation for the unfamiliar behavior. While these explanations varied somewhat from teacher to teacher, a common theme emerged. On several occasions unfamiliar and disturbing behavior (whether antisocial actions or difficulty mastering classroom work) was attributed to problems in a child's environment. Comments such as I think Ben is brutalized at home were offered as explanations for children's actions or attitudes. To a lesser extent I heard references made to children's previous schools not having demanded enough of them. Whether these expla-

nations accurately represented fact or not, they made the problems under-standable and to some extent served to legitimate the approach taken by the teachers to ameliorate the problems. (15, p. 21)

Because cultures express emotions and feelings in different nonver-bal ways, special education educators sometimes misjudge how stu-dents are feeling. European Americans typically express anger and defiance by silent stares. African Americans roll their eyes, and many Asian and Pacific Island Americans force a smile when they are angry. As Johnson explains, among African Americans, especially females,

> Rolling the eyes is a nonverbal way of expressing impudence and disapproval of the person who is in the authority role and of communicating every nega-tive label that can be applied to the dominant person. . . . Often white teach-ers (who are in an authority role and who have contact with Black children) will miss the message communicated by Black children when they roll their eyes. (14, pp. 18, 57)

African American (and Hispanic) females will also stand with their hand or hands on their hips when they are angry or defiant. Johnson advises that: "Most Black people know to 'cool it' when Black women take this stance. The nonverbal message communicated when a Black female takes this stance is: 'I'm really mad, now. You better quit mess-ing with me" (14, p. 57).

The ways African American, Asian and Pacific Island American, Hispanic American, and other students of color typically show respect and submission is different than the way European American students are expected to behave. As a result, European Americans often misin-terpret the lack of eye contact among their students of color. For exam-ple,

> Asians generally tend to use repeated head nodding, avoidance of direct eye contact, and minimal spontaneous verbalization, and to refrain from making critical comments, as a way of showing deference toward an authority figure. (16, p. 49)
>
> Occasional avoidance of eye contact by Oriental children may be classified as submissive behavior . . . such avoidance of eye contact provides others with a distorted image of an Oriental child—as being timid, shy, insecure, suspicious, undependable, and lacking self confidence. (18, p. 69)
>
> Avoidance of eye contact by a Black person communicates "I am in a sub-ordinate role and I respect your authority over me," while the dominant cul-

ture member may interpret avoidance of eye contact as "Here is a shifty, unreliable person I'm dealing with." (14, p. 18)

INDIVIDUALIZING CLASSROOM MANAGEMENT
TECHNIQUES

Exceptional students' cultural characteristics can affect the ways they respond to different classroom/behavior management styles, and as a result, the effectiveness of their teachers management techniques (19-32). The way students are accustomed to relating to adults at home and in their communities affects the way they perceive authority figures in school and the kinds of authority they are comfortable with. Although many experts advise teachers to be authoritative rather than authoritarian, students from cultures in which adults relate to children in an authoritarian manner may require help in adjusting to an adult who is authoritative and not authoritarian.

> In many instances white teachers are unable to discipline Black children because they do not "connect" culturally; the teachers do not behave as Black children expect authority figures to behave. . . . It seems that when white teachers practice the disciplinary techniques they are taught in college, Black children "run over them." (24, p. 172)

In a somewhat similar vein, Tharp advises that teachers of Hawaiian Americans need to be tough: "To be tough, the teachers must be firm, clear, and consistent in insisting that the children comply with their directions and requests. They must dispense contingently the resources they control, such as recess, access to peers, and praise" (31, pp. 354).

Students accustomed to authoritarian adults may also have difficulty participating in democratic classrooms in which the students are actively involved in establishing rules, procedures, and consequences. The difficulties some African American and Filipino American students can have adjusting to democratic classrooms is described in the following quotations.

> Those who are accustomed to a more authoritarian approach to behavior management are particularly difficult to control in an atmosphere of permissiveness, of being given freedom to choose prematurely and without training. (19, p. 7)

Especially to a small child from grade one to grade six, the democratic atmosphere that is being provided here is an entirely new aspect. Perhaps, during the first months the Filipino student is somewhat lost. He doesn't know what to do. The Filipino child may feel insecure. In the Philippines, the teacher usually says, "do this, make this." (22, p. 21)

In some cultures the authority roles of male and female adults are very different. In these cultures males typically are the authority figures and females are the nurturer. Students brought up in these cultures may not be ready to accept female teachers as authority figures or to accept their use of disciplinary techniques that in their cultures are used only by males. A Hispanic American educator offers the following comment about Hispanic American males' perceptions of their female teachers: "One should be conscious of a male Chicanos' lack of understanding in trying to take orders from a female teacher. He will really look up to or listen with better interest if an adult male is talking to him" (6, p. 127).

Adults from different cultural backgrounds use different techniques to motivate children and youth to behave in acceptable ways. Some ethnic groups rely heavily on the use of criticism and consequences to modify children's behavior; others do not. Some are quick to resort to punishments; others emphasize rewards. Therefore, it is helpful to know the kinds of disciplinary techniques that students are accustomed to in their homes and communities.

The amount of praise and rewards students receive from adults depends in part on their cultures. What is an unnecessary or excessive amount of praise for some students may be just the amount or less than what others are accustomed to receiving. Providing students with less than their customary amount of praise and rewards may cause them to think that their teachers do not value them or their work. On the other hand, rewarding and praising students excessively can cause them to become dependent.

Navajo adults are more reserved in their affectionate displays but are highly respectful of children's individuality and of children's sovereignty over their own persons. Punishment, contingent reward, or any openly manipulative effort to control the behavior of others—including children—is a violation of cultural values. (31, p. 354)

Cultures differ in the kinds of rewards they provide children. Some, like the European American culture, stress materialistic rewards;

other, like the Hispanic American culture, bring up children and youth to respond to more personal ones. In some cultures children strive for individual recognition, in others anonymity is preferred. Many students of color, especially Asian and Pacific Island Americans, Hawaiian Americans, Hispanic Americans, and Native Americans have such difficulty in classrooms that stress individual goals, and individual recognition that it is often better to recognize their achievement in a less public manner.

Some cultures reward individuals, others the group the individual belongs to. Because Hawaiian American students are very group oriented, rewarding individual Hawaiian American students for behaving well can cause them to behave in less desirable ways to avoid being singled out for praise and recognition. On the other hand, rewarding the whole group for the improvement of one or more members of the group can encourage those individuals who are not behaving appropriately to behave in a more desirable manner.

Culture also influences the kinds of negative consequences adults use to discipline youngsters—physical punishments (spanking and slapping), loss of affection (statements of disappointment and anger), loss of attention, or the possibility of social interaction (removal from the presence of others), loss of privileges (being grounded, loss of TV), or loss of material things (desserts, allowances). As a result, students from different cultural backgrounds experience the same negative consequences differently.

For example, because Hawaiian American children are used to spending much more time with their peers than are Navajo children, "'Time-out' from the social interaction of recess or in-class activities is a sharp punishment for Hawaiian children. In Navajo classrooms, children are quite content to be alone" (31, pp. 354-355).

Students who are accustomed to receiving negative feedback about their behavior only in private and never in public may react antagonistically when special education educators discipline them by writing their names on the blackboard or commenting about their inappropriate behavior in front of others.

Students from different cultural backgrounds may also react differently to the same type of criticism. Many Southeast Asian Americans and Filipino Americans and Hispanic Americans find European American authority figures to be overly frank and intense.

Correction of students mistakes must be done tactfully. Filipino students often have difficulty detaching themselves from their work and may view adverse comments as direct criticisms of themselves. . . . Filipino children are particularly sensitive to criticism. When embarrassed the child may withdraw and become uncooperative. The teacher may be frustrated in all attempts to discover what is wrong. (25, p. 19)

Hispanic parents tend to speak more politely and indirectly when they criticize or discipline their children. In the United States educators are much more gruff and direct with students. . . . Some Hispanic students, especially males, may interpret the gruff or more direct manner of Anglos as an indication that educators do not consider them worthy or deserving of a proper relationship. When educators speak to them in a matter-of-fact or authoritarian manner, they may feel insulted, angry, or resentful and lose respect for these educators and the desire to cooperate or conform. (6, p. 102)

DISCRIMINATION

As noted in previous chapters, many exceptional students are still treated in a discriminatory manner because of their ethnic, socioeconomic-class, linguistic, or contextual characteristics. Many regular education educators and special education educators have lower expectations for poor students and many groups of students of color, especially African American, Hispanic American, and Native American students. They tend to expect less of them, evaluate them lower than objective evidence warrants, praise and call on them less often, criticize them more often, use harsher and more punitive disciplinary techniques with them, and so on. No one knows the exact degree to which behavior problems in school are caused by such discrimination. However, it is inconceivable that the discriminatory manner in which many exceptional students are treated by their teachers does not affect their attitudes and behavior. The elimination of teacher prejudice is one of the most important steps special educators can take to eliminate disciplinary problems.

REFERENCES

These references describe contextual factors that can affect students behavior in school:

1. Matus, D. E. (1990). *Urban High School Classroom Management: A Humanistic Approach.* ERIC ED 395 049.
2. McCoy, C. B., & McCoy, H. V. (1987). Appalachian youth in cultural transition. In P. J. Obermiller & W. W. Philliber (Eds.), *Too Few Tomorrows: Urban Appalachians in the 1980's.* Boone, NC: Appalachian Consortium Press.
3. Olsen, L. (1988). *Crossing the Schoolhouse Border: Immigrant Students and the California Public Schools.* San Francisco: California Tomorrow.
4. To, C. (1979). *The Educational and Psychological Adjustment Problems of Asian Immigrant Youth and How Bilingual-Bicultural Education Can Help.* Paper presented at the annual conference of the National Association of Asian American and Pacific Island Education, San Francisco.
5. Ulibari, S. (1970). *Stereotypes and Caricatures.* Paper presented at the National Education Task Force de La Raza Staff Training Institute, Albuquerque.

Culturally-influenced behavior that may be problematic is discussed in these references:

6. Grossman, H. (1995). *Educating Hispanic Students: Implications for Instruction, Classroom Management, Counseling, and Assessment* (2nd ed.). Springfield, IL: Charles C Thomas Publisher, Ltd.
7. Irvine, J. J. (1991). *Black Students and School Failure: Policies, Practices, and Prescriptions.* New York: Praeger.
8. Kochman, T. (1981). *Black and White Styles in Conflict.* Chicago: University of Chicago Press.
9. Nguyen, L. D. (1986). Indochinese cross-cultural adjustment and communication. In M. Dao & H. Grossman (Eds.), *Identifying, Instructing and Rehabilitating Southeast Asian Students with Special Needs and Counseling Their Parents.* ERIC ED 273 068.

Examples of how special educators can take students' characteristics into consideration when they interpret their behavior are found in these references:

10. Dent, J. L. (1976). Assessing black children for mainstream placement. In R. L. Jones (Ed.), *Mainstreaming and the Minority Child.* Reston, VA: Council for Exceptional Children.
11. Gay, G. (1975). Cultural differences important in the education of Black children. *Momentum,* October, 30-33.
12. Gay, G., & Abrahams, R. D. (1973). Does the pot melt, boil, or brew? Black children and white assessment procedures. *Journal of School Psychology, 11*(4), 330-340.

13. Jaramillo, M. L. (1973). *Cautions When Working with the Culturally Different Child.* ERIC ED 115 622.

14. Johnson, K. R. (1971). Black kinetics: Some nonverbal communication patterns in the Black culture. *Florida Reporter,* Spring/Fall, 17-20, 57.

15. Kritek, W. J. (1979). Teachers' concerns in a desegregated school in Milwaukee. *Integrated Education, 17,* 19-24.

16. Matsuda, M. (1989). Working with Asian parents: Some communication strategies. *Topics in Language Disorders, 9*(3), 45-53.

17. Wong, M. K. (1978). Traditional Chinese culture and the behavior patterns of Chinese students in American classrooms. In *Second Annual Forum on Transcultural Adaptation (Proceedings): Asian Students in American Classrooms.* Chicago: Illinois Office of Education.

18. Yao, E. L. (1979) Implications of biculturalism for the learning process of middle-class Asian children in the United States. *Journal of Education, 16*(4), 61-72.

These references describe how to individualize classroom management techniques:

19. Bacon, M. M. (n.d.). *Coping Creatively with Adolescence: Culturally Relevant Behavior Management Strategies for the Twenty-First Century.* Unpublished manuscript. Palo Alto, CA: Palo Alto Unified School District.

20. Condon, E. C., Peters, J. Y., & Sueiro-Ross, C. (1979). *Special Education and the Hispanic Child: Cultural Perspectives.* Philadelphia: Temple University, Teacher Corps Mid-Atlantic Network.

21. Ford, B. A., Obiakor, F. E., & Patton, J. M. (1995). *Effective Education of African American Exceptional Learners: New Perspectives.* Austin, TX: Pro-Ed.

22. Geschwind, N. (1974). *Cross-Cultural Contrastive Analysis: An Exploratory Study.* Unpublished master's thesis, University of Hawaii, Honolulu.

23. Grossman, H. (1995). *Classroom Behavior Management in a Diverse Society* (2nd ed.). Mountain View, CA: Mayfield.

24. Hale-Benson, J. E. (1986). *Black Children: Their Roots, Culture, and Learning Styles.* (Rev. ed.). Baltimore: Johns Hopkins University Press.

25. Howells, G. N., & Sarabia, I. B. (1978). Education and the Pilipino Child. *Integrated Education, 16*(2), 17-20.

26. Koh, T., & Koh, S. D. (1982). A note on the psychological evaluation of Korean school children. *P/AAMHRC Research Review, 1*(3), 1-2.

27. Leggio, P. (n.d.). *Contrastive Patterns in Nonverbal Communication among Different Cultures.* Trenton, NJ: Office of Equal Opportunity, New Jersey State Department of Education.

28. Medicine, B. (1985). Child socialization among Native Americans: The Lakota (Sioux) in cultural context. In *Indian Studies.* Cheney WA: Eastern Washington University.

29. Patton, J. M. (1981). *A Critique of Externally Oriented Behavior Management Approaches as Applied to Exceptional Black Children.* ERIC ED 204 902.

30. Peterson, R. L.,& Ishi-Jordan, S. (Ed.) (1994). *Multicultural Issues in the Education of Students with Behavioral Problems.* Cambridge, MA: Brookline Books.

31. Tharp, G. (1989). Psychocultural variables and constants: Effects on teaching and learning in schools. *American Psychologist, 44*(2), 349-359.

32. Wolfram, W., & Adger, C. T. (1993). *Language Differences Across Dialects.* Baltimore: Baltimore City Public Schools.

Chapter 7

OVERCOMING OBSTACLES TO CHANGE

We know who the students are that are treated unjustly by the special education system and the specific ways that they are treated unfairly. We have the know-how and the resources to correct the problem. Nevertheless, many special education educators, administrators, and psychologists resist learning about students' socioeconomic, cultural, contextual, linguistic, and gender characteristics. Moreover, many of those who do have this knowledge are nevertheless reluctant to adapt their methods to students' needs. The reasons why they do not do the right thing include their lack of diversity, their prejudicial attitudes, their reluctance to rock the boat because of the risks involved, their unwillingness to expend the energy involved in teaching in a multicultural manner, and their lack of preparedness for working with the diverse students in our special education programs.

UNREPRESENTATIVE SPECIAL EDUCATORS

The teachers who staff our special education programs are not representative of the students they teach (1-5). Teachers from poor, non-middle-class or non-European American backgrounds are scarce and becoming more scarce. Although 32 percent of students in special education programs are students of color, only 14 percent of their teachers are individuals of color. Statistics indicate that the disproportionality in the ethnic background of special education teachers will be maintained if not increased.

Professors of education bear some of the responsibility for the lack of diversity among our special education educators. With some exceptions, professors spend little time recruiting non-middle-class students and students of color into their teacher preparation programs. When they do, they tend to choose students who have adopted a middle-class European American way of life. In addition, they often turn off many of the students who have not assimilated to the mainstream culture by using culturally and contextually inappropriate instructional, classroom management and assessment approaches.

The situation in the university where I taught is a good example. A number of my colleagues who were awarded federal funds to provide scholarships to "minority" and/or bilingual students to increase the number of non-European American and bilingual special education educators asked me what I did to recruit students for the programs I ran. When I told them that we sent letters to the more than one thousand school buildings in our service area, made presentations about our program in the local school districts and at meetings of the county education administrators, interviewed candidates at sites off campus that were convenient to their places of residence or work, followed up every inquiry with at least a telephone call, asked graduates of our program to contact prospective students to encourage them to apply, and so on, they thanked me, but implemented few, if any, of my suggestions. The end result in many cases was that their minimal recruitment efforts were unsuccessful. And they met their quotas with students who were technically "minorities" because they were Jewish, Japanese-American, and so on, but not actually members of underrepresented groups; or students who spoke German, French, or other languages that were not needed by the limited proficient English elementary and secondary students in the university's service area; or just "warm European American bodies" who were more interested in the tuition waivers the programs offered than in serving students of color and limited English proficient students with disabilities. To protect themselves and continue to receive the funds, they provided misleading information to the people in Washington who monitored whether the programs were achieving their objectives.

Special education professors must recruit into their teacher preparation programs individuals who are devoted to improving the education of all students—poor, migrant, immigrant, and rural students and students of color as well as middle-class European American students. The recruitment of bilingual individuals, people of color, and working-class European Americans should be given special attention because they tend to understand and appreciate the importance of students' cultural, contextual, and linguistic characteristics, to be more effective with a diverse group of exceptional students and to be less prejudiced toward them (6, 9).

Selecting candidates of color has other potential benefits as well. There is some evidence that the higher the ratio of teachers of color to European American teachers on the staff of a school district the less discriminatory treatment students of color receive and the less likely they are to be overrepresented in special education programs for students with mild and severe developmental disabilities and emotional disorders, and underrepresented in programs for students who are gifted and talented (7, 8).

UNMOTIVATED AND PREJUDICED SPECIAL EDUCATORS

During my forty years in special education, I have known a great many caring special education educators and special education educators in training who were dedicated to helping all children and struggling to achieve that goal. I am sure that there are many thousands more like them whom I have never met. Unfortunately, many other special education educators do not to want to know that their approaches are culturally, contextually, and linguistically inappropriate for some of their students. These educators may be comfortable with their accustomed way of doing things and/or unwilling to face the anxiety of not knowing how to adapt their approaches to their students' individual needs. Many of them just care less about students whose skin color, socioeconomic, ethnic, contextual, or linguistic backgrounds are different from their own than they care about students they identify with. As far as they are concerned, ignorance is bliss. These attitudes are understandable because they reflect the human condition. However, they are attitudes that must be corrected.

Some special education educators believe that doing the right thing is not worth risking their relationships with colleagues or their job security. They are right about the risks they will run. The changes that are required in adapting traditional special education to the needs of the diverse students in our schools are threatening to those who wish to maintain the status quo. The community and educational forces arrayed against bilingual special education, Ebonics, multicultural special education, nonbiased assessment, and so on are formidable. It is risky to take on an establishment that is satisfied with the status quo or unwilling to change things because of politics. However, it is a risk that special education educators are obligated to take because they have assumed the responsibility for their students' educations.

Finally, some special education educators are unwilling to commit themselves to the additional time and effort that they think would be involved in adapting their approaches to their students' diverse needs. They too are partially right. Adapting special education methods to students' diverse needs would require considerable work on their part, but not extra work. They would be merely doing what is necessary to perform their job the way it should be done. My personal belief is that these attitudes reflect the self-centeredness that all of us must battle against to one degree or another.

One of the ways I measure the effectiveness of the courses in diversity that I teach is to compare my students' responses at the outset and at the end of the semester to questions about how they think a variety of problematic classroom situations should be handled. When I do so, I repeatedly find that at the end of the course they are much more likely to believe that teachers should adapt their approaches to their students' individual needs. However, when I ask my students if they would actually make the adaptions they affirm are desirable, their answers are mixed. In general, they report that they have adapted or anticipate adapting many of their instructional techniques to their students' cultural, socioeconomic, contextual, and linguistic needs. That is unlikely to cause them problems. They are less willing to adapt their classroom management approaches to their students' individual needs because accepting certain kinds of behavior would make them very uncomfortable. Moreover, they are extremely unlikely to adapt their assessment approaches to their students' characteristics because that would create major waves with their colleagues and administrators. As many of them put it, albeit apologetically, "I wouldn't risk my job by refusing to administer a test even though I knew it was biased."

Having been fired from or asked to leave a number of jobs when I was younger, I know that the threat they experience is real. However, when I think about the students who they are miseducating, I am not very sympathetic to their concerns.

Although many special education educators are in favor of adapting educational techniques to students' individual needs, the attitudes of many others reflect the prejudices prevalent in society (10-18). One prejudicial attitude some educators have is their belief that the European American culture that prevails in the United States is superior to the supposedly disadvantaged or inferior cultures from which many students of color or their parents emigrated. Special education educators who believe this think that it would be disastrous to encourage students to maintain the inferior cultural characteristics that held back progress in the countries from which they or their parents emigrated. Instead, they maintain that they should encourage students of color and their parents to give up those cultural characteristics that have held back the progress of their native countries. Believing that the European American middle-class culture that currently prevails in school is a superior culture, these special education educators claim that students will learn more effectively if they assimilate to the learning and behavior styles that prevail in schools and use the school's values as a standard to judge themselves. As one person put it:

> People came to this country to better themselves. If their native cultures are so great, why did they have to immigrate? If they aren't willing to accept the values that have helped the United States have the largest economy and the highest standard of living then they should return to the countries from which they came and settle for the limited opportunities they provide. (12, p. 18)

This point of view is just another example of the prejudicial attitudes that students of color experience in our schools. Moreover, there is little evidence to support the hypothesis that students who assimilate learn more efficiently. In fact, there is evidence that the non-European students who are most likely to be well adjusted and to succeed both academically and vocationally are not those who reject their ethnic identity, rather those who identify with their own ethnic group (19-27).

The reasons why these students are better adjusted and more successful have not been well studied. Some possible explanations are the following:

- Students who maintain their cultural identity have more self-esteem and self-confidence than those who reject their cultural background.
- Students who are attempting to assimilate may experience conflicts with their parents as well as identity conflicts, resentment, anger, and rebelliousness, all of which can interfere with their learning.
- In comparison to monocultural students, bicultural students have a larger repertoire of learning strategies and coping techniques to apply to the tasks and challenges of school.

A second prejudicial notion that some special education educators support is that adapting their approaches to individual students' will contribute to people wanting to follow different laws, operate on the basis of different values and moralities, and so on. This idea is embodied in the following statements.

> We cannot survive as a culture with different laws for different people. Everyone must pay taxes, serve in the army, respect private property and the rights of others regardless of where they were born or what religion they profess. (12, p. 10)

Pluralism in our society has produced a moral climate that tells everyone to establish a sense of what is right and wrong *for you.* This trend has a way of blurring the limits of a moral code. In the educational arena this trend has produced a no-fault morality and relativistic values. . . . Schools, if they are to survive, must protect and articulate moral standards, ethical behavior, and historical principles of social cohesion. It is their function to teach the common beliefs that unite us as a free nation (18, pp. 15-16).

These concerns are based on the incorrect assumption that persons who favor pluralistic approaches believe in complete cultural relativism. Pluralists typically recommend that diversity should be balanced against higher and universal values (16, 17). Two examples of this position follow.

> Because each cultural group proceeds from a different context, we can never reach total agreement on the "best" or most appropriate ways in which to lead our lives... Nevertheless, it should also be stressed that above and beyond all cultures there are human and civil rights that need to be valued and maintained by all people. These rights guarantee that all human beings are treated with dignity, respect, and equality. Sometimes the values and behaviors of a group so seriously challenge these values that we are faced with a dilemma to reject it or to affirm the diversity it represents. If the values we as human beings hold most dear are ultimately based on extending rights rather than negating them, we must decide on the side of those more universal values. (16, pp. 278-279)
>
> I believe in a form of cultural pluralism in which universal and particularistic values would be dialectically balanced against each other. In particular, I believe that the universal values of equality, freedom, and democracy, which are among the most important values that have been promulgated under the concept of common school, should be balanced against the particularistic values associated with the maintenance of cultural diversity. But the freedom of an individual must be restrained to the extent that it imposes detrimentally on the freedom of others. Unfortunately, this two-sided nature of cultural pluralism is rarely underlined and, as a consequence, it is sometimes misunderstood as license for runaway ethnicity, rather than as a way of avoiding such ethnocentric behavior. (17, pp. 300-301)

The contention that accommodating to cultural differences in the classroom necessarily leads to having two or more national languages and different laws for different cultural groups is also incorrect. Instructing students in their native languages while they learn English, permitting them to work at their own pace, developing the kinds of interpersonal relationships with them that make them feel comfortable, allowing them to choose whether to behave competitively or cooperatively, and so on does not necessarily lead to adopting two or more national languages, moral codes, or sets of laws.

Special education educators who are prejudiced against some of their students or unwilling to adapt their approaches to their students for the reasons described earlier resort to a number of arguments to defend their positions.

1. *Adapting classroom approaches to students needs does not prepare them for the real world.* Some special education educators have convinced themselves that because the real world is not nearly as tolerant or as flexible as school, adapting educational approaches to students' individual characteristics and backgrounds does not prepare the students to function effectively in the mainstream European American dominated society. They maintain that because employers and others require individuals to conform to mainstream expectations and norms, accommodating to students' culturally influenced behavior patterns, learning styles, communication styles, concepts of punctuality, and so on dooms them to be uncompetitive and disadvantaged in the real world. This is the same argument that some educators give to justify teaching students to speak standard English.

   As I stated earlier, there is some truth to this concern. Americans do live in an imperfect society. Despite federal and state laws against discrimination, many people with supervisory and administrative power over others continue to expect and insist that those over whom they have influence conform to their culturally influenced standards. However, does that mean that educators should prepare their students to accept the prejudicial attitudes of these individuals? Again we must ask who has the right to decide whether students should be encouraged and helped to submit to such abuse, or to fight it—the students' teachers or the students themselves?

   Many exceptional students do not want to replace their values, attitudes, learning and behavior styles, and so on with those of the European American middle class. Requiring them to do so can cause them to become angry, resentful, suspicious, rebellious, and to tune out their teachers or drop out of school. If students believe that their culture is inferior or they agree that they should change their culturally influenced ways of functioning they may suffer a loss of self-esteem and self-confidence. Even if students want to change, it may be too difficult to accomplish, because it is no easy task to change one's lifestyle and values.

   There is a limited capability within each of us to modify the ethnic traits we absorb as children. We may change our accent or the way we smile but we cannot, intellectually or emotionally, change the multitude of traits that would have to be altered to change our basic ethnicity. (14, p. 20)

Even if students succeed in changing, their efforts can create serious problems and unwanted side effects for them. When students of color act in ways that are less natural to them than to European American middle-class students who were brought up from their earliest years to behave in these ways, students of color can become tense and nervous. They may experience the guilt, shame, and anxiety that often results from rejecting one's culture. Students who assimilate may suffer the loss of friendship and outright hostility from peers who accuse them of trying to be "coconuts," "oreos," or "bananas" (brown, black, or yellow on the outside and white on the inside). This is especially likely to happen if there is movement within the students' culture toward increasing the groups' cultural pride or if there is a history of conflict and oppression between the students' ethnic group and the European American power structure.

There is little reason to assume that assimilation can work. It has been tried for years with very little success. This concern was expressed quite some time ago by one of the pioneers in the field of multicultural education.

Schools' past efforts to acculturate culturally different children have failed miserably. These children as a whole are still not being educated, and the school system cannot continue to ignore its ethical, legal, moral, and professional responsibilities to accommodate children as they are. It is highly presumptuous for any school system to assume the responsibilities of acculturating children when the potential emotional consequences of forced acculturation are so pernicious. If most educators realized the way in which they risk the mental health of culturally different children by insisting on acculturating them, they would look more favorably on their potential role in developing a culturally pluralistic society. (10, p. 555)

2. *It is impossible to accommodate educational approaches to the cultural needs of the many cultural groups found in any particular school system or often within a particular classroom.* Many people do not believe that educators can accommodate their methods and techniques to the different cultural groups with whom they work. Some of their reasons are included in the following quotation.

My school district, the Los Angeles County School District, has over one hundred different language/culture groups. How can anyone be expected to know about all these different cultures, and how can anyone be expected to apply what they do know? From what I have been told during in-service training, what are appropriate teaching techniques for one group are inappropriate for another. How can I teach my Anglo students one way, my Latino students a second way, my Vietnamese students a third, my Korean students a fourth way, my Hmong, my Portuguese, etc., at the same time? Impossible! (12, p. 16)

It is factually incorrect to assert that each culture requires a unique educational approach. Alternative methods of instructing students, assessing students, organizing classrooms, and counseling parents are limited. For example, educators can encourage or require their students to work individually or in groups; they can motivate them through the use of competitive games or cooperative settings; they can allow them to work at their own pace or encourage them to work as quickly as possible; they can attempt to develop close personal relationships with them or maintain a "professional distance"; they can correct and criticize them in front of their peers or privately; they can encourage them to discuss controversial issues and express differences of opinion or emphasize similarities of experience and opinion; and they can teach abstract concepts or utilize methods that stress the concrete and learning by doing. Because educators are always choosing between alternatives as limited as those listed earlier, they can easily adapt their methodology to the cultural needs of their students.

3. *To treat some students differently than others is discriminatory.* Some special educators argue that because all people are basically the same they should be treated the same. Not to do so, in their opinion is unfair and discriminatory.

Although it is true that human beings are similar, they prefer success to failure, praise and recognition to criticism or condemnation, and acceptance and attention to rejection and inattention. However, peoples' behavior in these situations is influenced by different cultural veneers. They have different criteria for success. They find different forms of praise and recognition rewarding. They differ in terms of when, where, why, and how they are willing to accept criticism or condemnation. They express acceptance and rejection in their own culturally influenced ways. Therefore, if teachers expect all individuals to behave the same way and interpret everyone's behavior from a single culturally influenced point of view, they may fail to respond to the unique needs of many of their students.

In addition, the result of treating all students the same may be that those who do not fit the model used by their teachers are treated in a discriminatory manner: "When teachers ignore students' race and claim that they treat all children the same, they usually mean that their model of the ideal student is white and middle-class" (15, p. 54).

For example, Hilliard advises that educators who believe that providing students the same instructional techniques, classroom management approaches, and so on have the mistaken notion that they are treating them equally and being fair to them. However, they are not treating all students the same but are dealing with some students in a culturally appropriate manner and others in a biased manner (13). Hilliard suggests that there is a more valid way of treating students the same which is to provide all students with culturally appropriate educational approaches. According to him, although this may make it appear that students are being treated differently, they are actually being treated the same and in a nondiscriminatory manner.

4. *Cultural descriptions can lead to misleading overgeneralizations.* Some special educators are concerned that teachers may think that their knowledge of the typical cultural, contextual, and linguistic characteristics of a group is sufficient for them to understand an individual student or parent. The following statement expresses this concern.

There are many common stereotypes of the Hispanic person such as never being on time, being deeply religious, etc. Those who work with Hispanics should be aware of this and guard against a generalized, stereotyped view of those they work with. This is not to say that a specific stereotype (like being deeply religious) may not apply to an individual. Rather, the individual should always be dealt with as a unique human being who may or may not exhibit certain attitudes, habits, and beliefs. . . . Educators must recognize that children come to us from an infinitely varied array of backgrounds and not assume that all Hispanic students come from poor or Indian backgrounds. (12, p. 14)

The possibility of overgeneralization is an ever-present danger.

However, although it is extremely important to avoid misleading stereotypes and overgeneralizations about any group of students, such generalizations can be helpful. They can sensitize special education educators, psychologists, and others who work in schools to the possibility that their students may have certain stereotypic attitudes, preferences, values, learning styles, and behavior patterns. However, they should never assume that their students will necessarily think and behave in these ways. It is as important to avoid relating to students on the basis of incorrect stereotypes as it is to avoid being insensitive to the influence students' ethnic characteristics have on their attitudes and behavior.

5. *Treating groups of students differently can result in lower expectations and standards for them. It can also lead European Americans to retaliate against those who they believe are given preferential treatment.* These are valid concerns. In an attempt to be culturally, contextually, and linguistically relevant, some well-meaning special education educators do lower their standards for students. However, these teachers are not following the advice of experts who caution them to maintain realistic standards and expectations for students while they educate them in a culturally appropriate manner and not assume that they will misbehave or achieve less than others.

UNDERPREPARED EDUCATORS

During my thirty-some-odd years as a professor, I met some outstanding professors of special education who were dedicated to preparing their students to succeed with the diverse group of children with disabilities that attend our schools. Although most of them were people of color, quite a few were European Americans like myself. Unfortunately, these committed professors are not in the majority. In general, professors of special education do not prepare teachers to work with the diverse group of students enrolled in our special education programs. Many special education professors pay lip service to preparing educators to succeed with our diverse groups of students. They claim that they include multicultural approaches in the courses they teach. However, at best, they merely include one or two, occasionally three articles about multicultural education in their assigned readings, tell students not to be prejudiced, and let it go at that.

With few exceptions, professors do not select textbooks that have a multicultural approach for their courses. When they teach their students how to instruct, manage, counsel, and assess students they recommend the same techniques for all students. Moreover, when they themselves instruct and assess their own students and manage their own classrooms, they use the same techniques with all students without regard to the diversity among them. Typically they use their same preferred teaching styles whether it be lecturing, cooperative learning, small group discussion, and so on over and over again, never thinking that their students' have different learning styles. They often take students' participation in class discussions into account when determining their grades (sometimes telling students in advance how many points classroom participation will be worth) even though some students may not wish to talk in class, and even though there is no evidence that talking in class is related to learning. They give all their students the same multiple choice, or short or long essay test, without thinking about the possibility of providing students with alternative ways of demonstrating their competency. They assess all students with timed tests, even though some students may not be able to demonstrate what they have accomplished in the course when they are rushed. They often deduct points or lower the grade they give to a paper that is turned in late, completely disregarding the fact that the context of the lives of some of their students may have prevented them from completing the assignment "on time." And so on.

This intolerable situation must change. First, we need to hire more professors of color who are more likely to be sensitive to and appreciative of the influence of cultural, linguistic, contextual, and gender factors on all students' learning and behavior (28). This will require paying more than lip service to faculty diversity and giving priority to hiring professors of color or European American professors with the required experience and knowledge. My experience indicates that this will be an unpopular policy among some faculties. However, it is an absolutely essential one.

Even if faculty attitudes were to change overnight, as of now, the number of special education educators of color with doctorate degrees and doctoral students is insufficient to diversify our special education personnel preparation programs. Therefore, we must begin by recruiting more of them into our doctoral training programs. This will not be easy. In comparison to European American special education educators, special education educators' of color decisions about whether to pursue a doctorate degree are influenced by program support for tuition, books, and living expenses; the number of people of color on the faculty, among the students in the program, and in the local community; the services available to people of color; and the presence of organizations that concern themselves with their interests (29, 30). This suggests that universities and state and federal governments will have to provide the funding necessary to enable them to engage in doctoral studies. They will have to attract them in sufficient numbers that special education educators of color will feel welcome and comfortable, not isolated on university campuses.

Second, all professors of special education have to become knowledgeable about the ways in which teachers and professors can adapt their instructional, classroom management and assessment approaches to the specific different cultural, linguistic, and contextual characteristics of their students. Sensitivity to and appreciation of individual differences is a necessary first step, and, god knows a difficult one to achieve with higher education faculty. However, sensitivity is insufficient. As professors become knowledgeable about these differences and how to accommodate to them, they must act on their knowledge in their own classrooms. This means modeling the kinds of behavior that their students need to learn.

To begin with, they must have textbooks that have an honest-to-goodness multicultural approach for their courses. Unfortunately, it is not possible for professors to select textbooks for their courses that pay more than lip service to diversity. Although there are a few textbooks that can be used in courses that focus primarily on diversity issues in special education, almost none of the current textbooks that are designed for courses on instructional methods, curriculum, assessment, counseling, classroom management, and so on discuss how special educators can adapt the techniques they include to the diverse group of students that are served by special education programs. I know of no research that explains why textbooks writers and publishers do not produce books that deal adequately with diversity. However, it may well be that they believe that nonbiased education textbooks would be unprofitable because the European American professors who teach the courses at which they are aimed would not order them.

Professors of special education must also use a variety of techniques such as lecturing, cooperative learning, small group discussion, and so on to meet needs of their students and to model what is required to meet the needs of elementary and secondary school students. They must allow students to select from a variety of assessment approaches the ones that enable them to demonstrate their competency. They should maintain flexible schedules for turning in papers and other work and completing course requirements. And so on.

Practicing what they should preach by using a variety of assessment, instructional, and classroom management approaches in their own classrooms, will be a real challenge to professors of special education. Many of them will have to change their attitudes about multicultural education, their belief that academic freedom bestows on professors the right to decide how to instruct and evaluate their students, and their concern that doing the right thing is not worth risking their relationships with colleagues or their tenure and promotion.

For 16 years I directed a bilingual/multicultural special education personnel preparation program. Many a time, students would angrily and resentfully complain to me that they felt that they were studying in two different programs. The faculty who taught the courses in the bilingual/ multicultural program were emphasizing how to adapt their methodology to the ethnic, socioeconomic-class, contextual, and linguistic differences among students. However, diversity was seldom mentioned in their regular special education courses in which they were being taught that one method fits all students.

The last time I attended a conference of the Council for Exceptional Children, I made it a point to attend as many sessions that dealt with diversity as possible. What I saw was consistent and unfortunate: African American, Asian and Pacific Island American American, and Hispanic professors presenting to other African American, Asian and Pacific Island American, and Hispanic American professors and teachers. The situation had not changed very much since the 1960s. The people who had the greatest need to attend the sessions were elsewhere, participating in sessions that did not deal with diversity and that were not presented by professors of color.

For many years I was afraid that there might be something the matter with me that made me so critical of most of my colleagues. Why didn't I fit in at any of the universities I had worked in, I asked myself. Why didn't I attend the faculty social affairs? Why was I so angry with my colleagues? Why did they seem so self-centered and hypocritical? Who was I to put myself on a pedestal? Then I read a book about professors from working-class backgrounds that included the first-person descriptions of twenty-some-odd working-class professors' university experiences. With very few exceptions, their experiences were like mine. They too felt alienated and separated from their middle class colleagues. While many professors from working-class backgrounds described themselves as feeling guilty about leaving so many other working-class people behind and having a mission to improve the lot of working-class students, they found that their colleagues did not identify with their working class students, and were not realistic about their needs. Like me, they also believed that their colleagues were more interested in their careers—in being granted tenure, earning promotions, and improving their status by publishing research and making presentations at conferences, than in their students' education and welfare.

The realization that my feelings and beliefs were shared by others, and that I was not alone, helped me to deal better with the class conflicts I experienced. But it did not enable me to be more successful in my attempts to help my middle-class European American colleagues make their courses more relevant to teachers in training of color and from working-class backgrounds and the working class students and students of color they would be teaching.

Each semester I ask the students in the courses on diversity issues in special education what they would need to do a good job with a group of diverse students. Invariably, their lists include detailed information about their students' cultures and the context of their lives, knowledge about how to adapt their educational techniques to the cultural and contextual needs of their students, the motivation to work hard and long, and the strength to make changes that would probably be unpopular with their administrations and communities.

Professors need these things as well to adapt what they teach and how they teach it to the needs of our diverse students. Unfortunately, most professors lack the information and the motivation to do the job. My guess is that many of them probably would also lack the courage to use the information if they had it. As a result, professors are not providing teachers in training with the information and skills they require to enable all students to succeed in our schools. They certainly are not modeling the kind of teaching that is necessary to meet the needs of the diverse group of students in America's schools and to bring about educational equality. Thus, until professors of special education become more representative of the students in the schools, and European American professors commit themselves to preparing teachers to succeed with all students in our schools, the current level of teacher unpreparedness will probably continue or worsen.

Special education personnel preparation programs should offer multicultural preparation. Most special education educators know very little about how their poor students and students of color live. To correct this, teacher training programs have to provide future teachers with firsthand experience with them (31). As Ewing points out,

> Improving school outcomes for African American children requires taking brave, bold, unusual steps. . . . Until there is a wholehearted acceptance of the idea that major changes must occur in teacher education to improve schools for African American children, there is little promise for ameliorating the intensifying debacle currently facing the nation . . . teacher education programs must excel in preparing teachers and administrators who have an elevated level of authentic knowledge of African American culture; a deeper understanding of the impact African American culture has on behavior, learning styles, and preferred teaching styles; and a genuine appreciation for the valuable repertoire of experiences African American children bring to school . . . . preservice students must be immersed in extended, direct, real-life experiences in the African American milieu. Useful resources for gaining experiences, knowledge, and appreciation for African American cultural treasures systematically neglected in our schools include summer community-based programs; after-school community-based student and parent learning centers; student teaching experiences Big Brother-Big-Sister programs; Urban League and NAACP community programs; and church-affiliated elder care, preschool day care, and after-school child care programs. (32, pp. 198-199)

In an ideal world, Ewing's statements would be followed by personnel preparation programs that prepare teachers to work with students from other ethnic backgrounds and students who are immigrants, migrants, homeless, and so on. However, in the less-than-ideal world in which we live, it would be impossible to provide teachers with the experiences they need to work effectively with all the different groups of diverse students in our schools. At the very least however, teacher preparation programs should target a few of the groups that are represented in their service areas and provide their students with intensive experience with these groups. Equally important, teacher preparation programs must teach educators the truth about prejudice and how to combat it. Until we eliminate the prejudice that infects our society, we will not be able to eliminate the prejudice in our school system that contributes so mightily to educational inequality. This will require identifying the specific courses in which these topics should be studied and monitoring to make sure that they are.

Finally, programs should prepare educators to be change agents rather than fit-ins because the status quo in schools is unacceptable. Students, especially those that are the victims of prejudice, must also be taught how to resist and combat it. This goal will not be very popular among professors. Most professors would agree that teachers' expectations for students, evaluation procedures, instructional techniques, curriculum materials, and classroom management techniques should be as free from bias as possible. However, they are unlikely to buck the system by modeling unbiased practices in their own classrooms. Professors learn early in their careers that fitting in is the way to survive and get ahead at most institutions of higher education. Professors who have learned this lesson and who possess personalities necessary to put it into practice will have difficulty preaching the opposite to their students.

CONCLUDING COMMENTS

All special education educators can and should contribute to making the special education system more equitable for poor, immigrant, refugee, migrant, rural, limited English proficient students, and students of color. Because middle-class European American professionals compose the preponderance of those who staff special education programs, they can do the most to correct it. Some of them are doing all in their power to do so; the majority are not. The question is whether these others will have the strength to face their shortcomings, especially their prejudice and ignorance, the humanity required to adapt the special education system to the needs of students who are least like them, and the commitment required to devote the additional time and effort that these adaptations necessitate.

Special education educators of color who understand from experience the neglect and discriminatory treatment described in this book have a pivotal role to play in the improvement of our special education system. They are in the best positions to inform and educate their European American colleagues about its true nature and to model the behavior necessary to correct it. For special education educators of color to do so takes a great deal of courage because in our prejudiced society, they risk alienating their colleagues with whom they have to work and on whom they have to depend for tenure, promotions, and the like. Despite these risks, many of them are doing all they can to change things. Others, however, need to increase their efforts. The question is whether they will dare to do so.

I do not want to add my voice to those calling for tokenism and half-hearted changes that do not benefit students sufficiently. Halfway solutions are insufficient solutions. Although none of us can contribute more than partially to the solution of the inequality in special education, we all must aim for a complete solution. That is the only way we will accomplish the whole task. If we all do our part, we can move mountains.

It is easy for special education educators to say that change is an evolutionary process that proceeds slowly, or to claim that inequality always has been and always will be with us because we cannot change human nature. However, special educators do not have the right to adopt such an attitude. People who are not suffering injustice should not be pointing to the progress that the previous generation made and telling today's exceptional students and their parents to be patient. Why should they be patient? They are suffering injustice. What right do people have to ask them to settle for a half a loaf even for a little while, if they are not suffering the same injustices and are eating from a full loaf? Slow and steady progress is not good enough. The elimination of inequalities in special education has to be not only rapid and continuous, but as immediate and complete as possible.

REFERENCES

These references indicate that special education educators are not and may continue not to be representative of the diverse group of students they serve:

1. American Association of Colleges for Teacher Education. (1994). *Teacher Education Pipeline III: Schools, Colleges, and Department of Education Enrollments by Race, Ethnicity, and Gender.* Washington, DC: Author.
2. Cook, L. H., & Boe, E. E. (1995). Who is teaching students with disabilities? *TEACHING Exceptional Children, 28*(1), 70-72.
3. National Clearinghouse for Professionals in Special Education. (1996). *A Summary of DPP Funding for Fiscal Year 1995.* Reston VA: Council for Exceptional Children.
4. U. S. Department of Education, Office of Special Education Programs. (1994). *Seventeenth Annual Report to Congress on the Implementation of the Individuals with Disabilities Education Act.* Washington, DC: Author.
5. Wald, J. (1996). *Culturally and Linguistically Diverse Populations in Special Education: A Demographic Analysis.* Reston, VA: Council for Exceptional Children.

References that document the advantages of increasing the number of faculty of color are listed next:

6. Grant, L. (1984). Black females' "place" in desegregated classrooms. *Sociology of Education, 57,* 98-110.
7. Meier, K. J., Stewart, J. Jr., & England, R. E. (1989). *Race, Class, and Education: The Politics of Second-Generation Discrimination.* Madison: University of Wisconsin Press.
8. Serwatka, T. S., Deering, S., & Grant, P. (1995). Disproportionate representation of African Americans in emotionally handicapped classes. *Journal of Black Studies, 25*(4), 492-506.
9. Simpson, A. W., & Erickson, M. T. (1983). Teachers' verbal and nonverbal communication patterns as a function of teacher race, student gender and student race. *American Educational Research Journal, 20*(2), 183-198.

The following references discuss the pros and cons of adapting educational techniques to students' individual needs and reasons why some special educators and psychologists do so and others do not:

10. Bernal, E. (1974). A dialogue on cultural implications for learning. *Exceptional Children, 40,* 552-563.
11. Graybill, S. W. (1997). Questions of race and culture: How they relate to the classroom for African American students. *Clearing House, 70*(6), 311-318.
12. Grossman, H. (1995). *Educating Hispanic Students: Implications for Instruction, Classroom Management, Counseling, and Assessment* (2nd ed.). Springfield, IL: Charles C Thomas Publishers, Ltd.

13. Hilliard III, A. G. (1992). *Language, Culture, and Valid Teaching.* Paper presented at the Topical Conference on Cultural and Linguistically Diverse Exceptional Children. Minneapolis.

14. Irvine, J. J. (1991). *Black Students and School Failure: Policies, Practices, and Prescriptions.* New York: Praeger.

15. Longstreet, W. S. (1978). *Aspects of Ethnicity.* New York: Teachers College Press.

16. Nieto, S. (1992). *Affirming Diversity: The Sociopolitical Context of Multicultural Education.* New York: Longman.

17. Suzuki, B. H. (1984). Curriculum transformation for multicultural education. *Education and Urban Society, 16,* 294-322.

18. Thomas, M. D. (1981). *Pluralism Gone Mad.* Bloomington, IN: Phi Delta Kappa Educational Foundation.

These references provide evidence that students who maintain their culture tend to be better adjusted:

19. Buriel, R. (1984). Integration with traditional Mexican-American culture and sociocultural adjustment. In J. L. Martinez Jr. & R. H. Mendoza (Eds.) *Chicano Psychology* (2nd ed.) Orlando, FL: Academic Press.

20. Buriel, R., & Saenz, E. (1980). Psychocultural characteristics of college bound and non-college bound Chicanos. *Journal of Social Psychology, 110,* 245-251.

21. Cloud, N. (1991). Acculturation of ethnic minorities. In A. M. Ambert (Ed.), *Bilingual Education and English as a Second Language: A Research Handbook 1988-1990.* New York: Garland.

22. Landsman, M., Padilla, A., Clark, C., Liederman, H., Ritter, P., & Dornbusch, S. (1990). *Biculturality and Academic Achievement among Asian and Hispanic Adolescents.* Paper presented at the annual meeting of the National Association for Bilingual Education, Tuscon.

23. Santiseban, D., & Szapocznik, J. (1982). Substance abuse disorders among Hispanics: A focus on prevention. In R. M. Becerra, M. Karno, & J. I. Escobar (Eds.), *Mental Health and Hispanics: Clinical Perspectives.* New York: Grune & Stratton.

24. So, A. Y. (1987). High-achieving disadvantages students: A study of low SES Hispanic language minority students. *Urban Education, 22*(1), 19-35.

25. Szapocznik, J., Kurtines, W. M., & Fernandez, T. (1979). *Bicultural Involvement and Adjustment in Hispanic Youths.* ERIC ED 193 374.

26. Torres-Matrullo, C. M. (1980). Acculturation, sex-role values and mental health among mainland Puerto Ricans. In A. M. Padilla (Ed.), *Acculturation: Theory, Models, and Some New Findings.* Boulder, CO: Westview Press.

27. Vigil, J. D. (1982). Chicano high schoolers: Educational performance and acculturation. *Educational Forum, 47*(1), 58-73.

This reference indicates that the vast majority of teacher trainers are European American:

28. Zimpher, N., & Ashburn, E. (1992). Countering parochialism in teacher candidates. In M. Dilworth (Ed.), *Diversity in Teacher Education*. San Francisco: Jossey-Bass.

Information about the factors that influence educators' decisions about whether to enroll in doctorate programs is found in these publications:

29. Boone, R. S., & Ruhl, K. L. (1995). Controllable factors in recruitment of minority and non minority individuals for doctoral study in special education. In B. A. Ford (Ed.), *Multiple Voices for Ethnically Diverse Exceptional Learners*. Reston, VA: Council for Exceptional Children.
30. Wright, D. J. (1987). Minority students: Developmental beginnings. In D. J. Wright (Ed.), *Responding to the Needs of Today's Minority Students*. San Francisco: Jossey-Bass.

Evidence of the positive effects of practical teaching experience with ethnically different exceptional students is found in the following reference:

31. Minner, S., & Prater G. (1994). *Preparing Special Educators for Work in Rural Areas. Two Field-Based Programs That Work*. ERIC ED 369 612.

The quote about providing special educators with meaningful life experiences with African American exceptional students is found in this publication:

32. Ewing, N. J. (1994). Restructured teacher education for inclusiveness: A dream deferred for African American children. In B. A. Ford, F. E. Obiakor, & J. E. Patton (Eds.), *Effective Education of African American Exceptional Learners*. Austin, TX: Pro-Ed.

Please remember that this is a library book,
and that it belongs only temporarily to each
person who uses it. Be considerate. Do
not write in this, or any, library book.

DATE DUE

MR 22 '03			
AP 13 '03			
DE 11 '03			
JY 16 '04			
OC 26 04			
AP 11 '05			
JE 13 '05			
MR 09 '07			
8/8/10			